Whatever Happened to the Egyptians?

Whatever Happened to the Egyptians?

Changes in Egyptian Society
from 1950 to the Present

Galal Amin

Illustrations by Golo

The American University in Cairo Press
Cairo • New York

Seventh printing 2004

An earlier version of this book was published in Arabic in 1998
as *Madha hadatha li-l-Misriyin?*
Protected under the Berne Convention

An earlier version of chapter 1 appeared in Charles Tripp and
Roger Owen, eds., *Egypt under Mubarak,* London: Routledge,
1989. Reproduced by permission.

An earlier version of chapter 2 appeared in Galal Amin, *Egypt's
Economic Predicament: A Study in the Interaction of External
Pressure, Political Folly and Social Tension in Egypt, 1960–1990,*
Leiden: E.J. Brill, 1995. Reproduced by permission.

An earlier version of chapter 13 appeared in "The Development
of Social Science in Egypt," *Cairo Papers in Social Science,* Fifth
Annual Symposium, vol. 18, No. 3, Cairo: The American
University in Cairo Press, 1995.

Dar el Kutub No. 14351/99
ISBN 977 424 559 8

Designed by the AUC Press Design Center
Printed in Egypt

Contents

"If, beginning with the eleventh century, we examine what has happened in France from one half-century to another, we shall not fail to perceive that at the end of each of these periods a two-fold revolution has taken place in the state of society. The noble has gone down the social ladder, and the commoner has gone up; the one descends as the other rises. Every half-century brings them nearer to each other, and they will soon meet. Nor is this peculiar to France. The various occurrences of national existence have everywhere been turned to the advantage of democracy, all men have aided it by their exertions, both those who have intentionally labored in its cause and those who have served it unwittingly; those who have fought for it and even those who have declared themselves its opponents have all been driven along in the same direction..."

Alexis de Tocqueville,
Democracy in America, 1835

Introduction

In 1996, the Egyptian monthly journal *al-Hilal* decided to dedicate a section of each issue to a discussion of the question 'Whatever Happened to the Egyptians?,' asking a number of its writers to contribute their opinions from any perspective they might choose. As we were on the threshold of the twenty-first century, the editor of *al-Hilal* deemed it fitting that we contemplate the changes that had taken place in Egyptian social life.

I welcomed the opportunity to participate in the discussion and chose to write about the changes that I had observed in the status of women in Egypt over the past fifty years. I thought of comparing the status of three generations of women in my own family, my mother, my two sisters, and my daughter. I tried to make use of my own personal experience as well as of the knowledge I had acquired from my academic studies and my readings on the development of the Egyptian economy and society, hoping that my experience of the specific would increase my understanding of the general, and vice versa. Having started with the subject of the status of women, I moved on to one aspect of Egyptian society after another, and the result was a collection of essays that make the bulk of this book.

Each time I wrote on one aspect or another of the development of Egyptian society over the last fifty years, I found my attention drawn to the role played by the high rate of social mobility experienced by Egypt during this period. This did not surprise me. For one thing, social mobility, or the degree to which different classes or sections of the population move upward or downward in relation to each other over time, seems to be intimately connected with the most powerful of the social forces that drive us, such as the desire to acquire the esteem and respect of others, the urge to prove oneself superior or to dominate, and the fear of losing any of these. Perhaps then, the nature of social mobility and the rate at which it accelerates or decelerates reveals as much about society at large as such urges and desires reveal about many aspects of individual behavior. If it is also true, as seems to be the case, that the rate of social mobility during the last fifty years has been higher than anything experienced by Egypt in its modern history, then, one may argue that social mobility could be the most important single factor behind many of the social changes that have occurred in Egypt since 1950.

And indeed, when I read over the articles I had written for the different issues of *al-Hilal* in 1996 and 1997, I was struck by how prominent this single factor had been in my thinking about almost every aspect of Egyptian social life. So I thought it appropriate to add to the collection two longer articles I wrote in 1985 on the causes and effects of rapid social mobility in Egypt. These stand as a more analytical introduction to the main body of articles.

My feeling is that the book has not suffered from its mixture of academic analysis and personal observation, and may have even benefited from it. I hope the reader will not think otherwise.

What is now in the reader's hands is a translation of the Arabic text which first appeared in January 1998 and was reprinted the following year. The translation is the work of three persons. An American friend, who is also an orientalist with a perfect command of the Arabic language, produced an English text very faithful to the original. I then made what appeared to me necessary changes to make it more readable for non-Arabs; finally my wife, Jan, read the whole text word by word, and introduced further improvements in style and gave me some good advice on substance. The result is a slightly shorter version than what appeared in Arabic, but maybe, at least for that reason alone, a better one.

Galal Amin
July 2000

1

Social Mobility

For some years now, Egyptians have been expressing a feeling of discontent, whether on the subject of the performance of the Egyptian economy, the state of culture and intellectual life, social relationships, morality, or political developments—whether domestic or in relation to other Arab or foreign countries.

Egyptian economists have been complaining about imbalances and distortions: a severe deficit in the balance of payments and a growing external debt, an imbalance in the state budget, and an output and employment structure too heavily dominated by the service sectors. Saving and investment ratios may indeed have reached unusually

7

high levels between 1975 and 1985 but both were caused by a big rise in unreliable and insecure sources of foreign exchange: oil exports, remittances of Egyptians working abroad, the Suez Canal and tourism, and in any case this rise came to an abrupt end in the late 1980s. Too much consumption, it is often said, is wasted on luxury imports and too much investment goes into 'unproductive' channels such as luxury housing and the import trade.

Egyptian sociologists have a similar list of complaints. Corruption and disrespect for the law are widespread and there is a conspicuous lack of work ethic. Violence is on the increase and previously unknown types of crime are spreading. Material values are establishing themselves, while productive and socially useful labor is losing social status and prestige. The quality of life in the city is rapidly deteriorating with increasing air pollution, overcrowding, congestion, noise and ugliness, while the village is rapidly changing from being a unit of production to one of consumption. In both the city and the village, there is an increasing westernization of social life accompanied by a growing respect for whatever is foreign and a disdain for everything local.

Political commentators, in their turn, complain that people's sense of loyalty and of belonging to the homeland has weakened, and that a preoccupation with the problems of everyday life has replaced what is often called a 'commitment to a project of national revival and progress,' or an interest in Arab nationalism. They also condemn the growing political and economic dependence on the United States.

Finally, those concerned with intellectual life and national culture point to the spread of what is regarded as 'low culture': the growth of fanaticism in religious movements and their excessive concern for ritualistic behavior; the decline of the Arab language as a means of expression in the mass media and the deterioration of the quality of education at all levels.

The most common explanation for these various manifestations of economic, social, political, and intellectual malaise is to blame them on the economic and political reorientation of Egypt in the early 1970s toward what is known as Infitah, or 'Open-Door' policies. This term is usually understood to mean three things: the opening of virtually all doors to the importation of foreign goods and capital, the removal of restrictions on Egyptian local investment, and the gradual withdrawal of the state from an active role in the economy. Many observers of the Egyptian scene find it easy to trace most of the problems listed above to this reorientation toward Infitah. The deficit in the balance of payments is attributed to the excessive liberalization of imports, the deterioration in income distribution is explained by the decline in state protection of the poor as well as by the excessive leniency of the authorities toward taxpayers, while the distorted economic structure is traced to the abandonment by the state of its role as an active investor in agriculture and industry and as a regulator of private investors. So many of the social, political, and cultural problems are said to be connected with growing inequality in income distribution which in its turn is attributed to Infitah.

While this explanation may touch upon an important part of the truth, one is inclined to think that it does not go to the heart of the matter. For whatever meaning may be attached to Infitah, it amounts essentially to a *negative* policy of removing restrictions and eradicating barriers, rather than forcing certain actions or initiating certain types of behavior. Economic liberalization simply *allows* consumers, investors, importers, and exporters to behave in a certain way, but does not by itself *create* the motive or inclination for such behavior. What I have in mind is something like the saying "You can lead a horse to water but you can't make it drink," and it is this desire to drink, or the lack of it, which I regard as the missing link between economic liberalization and the various aspects of economic and social behavior set out above. To give one example of what I mean, economic liberalization may indeed make the consumption or importing of certain goods possible, but it does not so easily make them desirable. Their desirability is more directly influenced by the levels of income of potential consumers and these people's position on the social ladder. The same policy of economic liberalization could not therefore be expected to produce the same results in two countries, say Egypt and China, with different social structures, levels of income, historical backgrounds, and psychological characteristics. My main argument in this chapter is that many of the manifestations of an economic and social 'crisis' in Egypt could be more convincingly attributed to the change in Egypt's social structure and to a rapid rate of social mobility which has been proceeding at a very accelerated pace over the last thirty years, than to the mere change in economic policy in the 1970s toward Infitah.

Economic liberalization may have itself been one of the main factors accelerating the rate of social mobility, but it has by no means been the only one. Important factors were at work long before the 1970s, while other factors which may have first appeared in that decade, could easily have occurred under a very different economic system. If this argument is correct, it would be quite wrong to imagine that the mere reversal of the policy of economic liberalization could by itself bring this 'crisis' to an end. Similarly, it would also be wrong to imagine that the current crisis will necessarily persist so long as economic liberalization continues.

Before I embark on substantiating my argument, I would like to point out how little attention has been given by economists and sociologists alike to the economic and social impact of the rapid change in Egypt's social structure. It is tempting to think of this as an example of an important area of investigation being neglected because it falls on the borderline between two disciplines—the economists leaving it to the sociologists and vice versa. The nearest that economists come to a discussion of this issue is when they tackle income distribution, but even if they were to have comparable data on personal or functional income distribution over a long period of time, which do not exist for Egypt, such data would reveal hardly anything of the changes that occurred in the social structure. The rise or fall in the share of say, the top 5 percent or the bottom 20 percent of the population, would tell us nothing about whether the members of any particular group have risen or fallen in relative income or social status or about the changes that might have occurred in their sources of income. Similarly, a rise or fall in the share of wages, in contrast to income from property, would tell us nothing about whether some wage earners may have now become property owners or vice versa. Such figures on the changes in personal or functional distribution of income are 'dead' figures, which may be appropriate in describing a change in chemical or physical phenomena but not that occurring in a living organism such as a society.

Likewise, sociological writings have unfortunately contributed very little to our understanding of the impact of social mobility on Egypt's current economic or social problems. Much has been written on the changes in social values and in patterns of behavior associated with economic liberalization or labor migration, and frequent references are made to the deterioration in work ethics, the spread of materialistic values and the growth of political apathy mentioned above. But hardly any attempt is made to show exactly how migration or economic liberalization could be responsible for these changes. When social mobility is discussed, the concern is usually with providing some indicators of the degree of the change in social structure rather than with its possible relationship to other aspects of economic and social life. Thus, Saad Eddin Ibrahim's pioneering essay "Social Mobility and Income Distribution in Egypt"[1] provides us with a wealth of statistics related to the rate of social mobility in Egypt between 1952 and 1979 and discusses some of its possible causes, but says virtually nothing about its impact. Moreover, considering the nature of available data and the lack of any standard for comparison, even the indicators provided in this essay leave us unable to judge whether the rate of social mobility has been 'high' or 'low.' To be told, for instance, that in 1979 the parents of 34 percent of Egypt's professionals had worked in agriculture[2] is of very little informative value in the absence of any corresponding percentage for an earlier date or for another country.

What is perhaps particularly disappointing is the way Marxist writers in Egypt deal with the phenomenon of social mobility, since one would expect them to be more concerned than most with the impact of class structure on the various aspects of political and social 'superstructure.' Egyptian Marxists however, seem to be mainly concerned with the division of Egyptian society into the 'exploited' and 'exploiting' classes, or into the 'productive' classes and the 'parasites.' That important sections of the traditionally down-trodden classes may have improved in social status over the last few decades is quickly dismissed with the emphasis that much of the new income of these newly wealthy individuals originates abroad or in 'unproductive' activities, while the fact that some sections of the upper classes may have suffered a decline in their income and social status is glossed over with an emphasis on the fact that new 'exploiters' have taken their places. Both types of observation may be true, but may also be no more interesting than the improvement that seems to have occurred in the standard of living of many of the poor and the decline in the economic and social standing of many of the rich.

The reader may be familiar with the variety of factors that contributed to the rise in the rate of social mobility in Egypt during the Nasserist era of the 1950s and 1960s, including the successive land reform laws between 1952 and 1961, the nationalization and sequestration measures of the early 1960s, the raising of minimum wages and of the rates of income tax, as well as the very rapid expansion of free education and other social services. To this one must also add the rapid increase in the rate of investment in agriculture and industry from 1957 to 1965, which led to the absorption of large numbers of agricultural surplus labor in irrigation projects, particularly in building the High Dam, and in manufacturing and construction work in the cities. The sheer growth of the role of the army and government in the economic, social, and political life of the country was itself a factor contributing to greater social mobility. From 1952 onward, the military establishment became a new and important channel of social advancement, while the growth of bureaucracy and of government-created political organizations provided new career ladders for a great number of university graduates who could not be absorbed in agriculture or industry.

While several of these factors lost much of their strength in the 1970s with the gradual abandonment by

the government of Nasser's 'socialist' policies, it is striking, and to some degree ironic, that the era of *laissez-
faire* of the 1970s seems to have witnessed a much higher rate of social mobility than that of the Nasserist era of
'Arab Socialism.' This is partly because, in spite of Sadat's
weak commitment to the welfare state, no government
during his rule could stand against the pressure of
demand for rapid expansion in school and university
enrollment. In fact, the expansion of university education
was faster in the 1970s than it had been in the 1950s and
1960s, and probably went much further toward reaching
the lower income groups of the population through the
rapid expansion of university education in the provinces.
Similarly, in spite of all the 1970s rhetoric claiming a
commitment to peace and declaring the war of October
1973 to be 'the last war,' the military establishment
showed no sign of slowing down its growth, either in size
or in acquiring privileges. Both the education and military establishments continued, therefore, to function as
channels for social advancement, but to these old channels the decade of the 1970s added some new channels of
its own. One of these, which gained much greater importance with the coming of the Infitah, was employment,
directly or indirectly, in the service of foreigners. Such
opportunities, which were extremely limited under
Nasser's more closed economy, came increasingly to be
extended further down the social scale. Thus, as well as
the professionals who worked in foreign companies,
banks, and consultancy offices, there were larger numbers of people from more humble social origins who

joined the service of foreigners in the flourishing tourist sector, import trade, real estate, or by providing a variety of personal services. Apart from realizing higher incomes than would have been possible from work in Egyptian institutions, work in the service of foreigners could bring with it new symbols of social advancement, such as acquiring some knowledge of a foreign language, the wearing of a uniform, or merely carrying the name of an illustrious foreign firm.

Two much more important factors, however, contributed to the acceleration of the rate of social mobility during the 1970s, namely external migration and the rise in the rate of inflation. Although the rate of external migration rose significantly toward the late 1960s, it did not start to contribute significantly to social mobility until the mid-1970s. Before this date, most Egyptian migrants belonged to relatively high income groups and were usually professionals, administrators, and high-level technicians. After 1974, the structure of Egyptian migration changed significantly, however, becoming increasingly dominated by unskilled and semi-skilled construction workers, craftsmen, and agricultural laborers migrating to the oil-rich countries of the Gulf. In contrast to other channels of social mobility, labor migration had a unique feature in that it required very little education and hardly any capital. It now offered opportunities for social advancement to the virtually illiterate, and demanded no more capital than the price of an air ticket which could be borrowed and repaid out of the earnings of the first few months in the new country.

Another contributor to social mobility in the 1970s was the sudden acceleration of the rate of inflation, which ranged between 20 percent and 30 percent in the years following 1974, compared with no more than 5 to 6 percent during the previous two decades. Many of the beneficiaries of inflation were among the already better off: the owners of large amounts of agricultural land or urban property, who benefited from soaring land prices and the rents of furnished apartments; the owners of industrial and commercial enterprises; contractors; and well-established, self-employed professionals. But there were also significant sections of the population that traditionally belonged to the lower income groups who benefited from inflation, such as the large number of craftsmen, construction workers, and agricultural laborers who were not themselves among the migrants but realized a rise in their real income as a result of the labor shortages created by migration. On the other hand, while inflation certainly hit the small landholders, the people in retirement, the unemployed, and the large number of lower-level government employees and public sector workers, it also lowered the real income of a significant section of the middle class consisting of government officials and professionals working in the public sector, as well as many of the new university graduates who failed to migrate or to find work in the newly established companies associated with the Infitah.

The impact of inflation on social mobility was not confined, however, to its effect on the relative real income from the *existing* occupations of various social groups; it also created new sources of income. To appreciate the importance of this fact, one needs only think, for example, of the ex-army officer who left his job to work in an import–export office, the small government employee who started working as a taxi driver in his spare time, the absentee landowner who started to cultivate his land for his own benefit, the craftsman becoming a small contractor, or the owner of a modest urban property who discovered the possibility of renting his furnished flat to an Arab tourist, and so on.

All these factors have worked together during the last three decades to bring about a rate of social mobility probably greater than anything Egypt has experienced in its modern history. They pushed large numbers of the population up the social ladder, who traditionally had belonged to the lowest levels of society and allowed them to compete successfully with sections of the middle class who found their social status rapidly declining. It will now be argued that the resulting change in social structure explains much more of the current economic, social, and intellectual scene than is usually recognized.

Egyptian economists have long complained of the tendency toward lavish consumption associated with the open-door policies of the 1970s. They have pointed to a sudden wave of consumerism symbolized by the rapid increase in the importation of motor cars, color TV and video sets, washing machines, air conditioners, American refrigerators, and Japanese fans. The objection is that this type of consumption is 'unnecessary,' 'wasteful,' and 'costly,' in so

far as it takes place at the expense of saving and investment, and creates too heavy a burden on the balance of
payments. Economists also observe that too much public
investment goes into infrastructure projects for the
benefit of high-income urban dwellers. It should be noted,
however, that what may be regarded as 'wasteful' when
looked at from the point of view of society as a whole,
could be regarded as perfectly acceptable from the point
of view of certain sections of that society that have just
experienced a big change in their social status. So many
of the goods and services consumed or aspired to by the
newly rising classes do not merely satisfy certain consumption needs but serve a much more important social
function as symbols of social advancement. To these
newly rising classes, the private motor car is not simply a
means of transport but also a status symbol that declares
their ascendance to a higher social level. Much of the
increase in luxury imports and the resulting burden in the
balance of payments can similarly be attributed not just
to an increase in income but also to the increase in social
mobility associated with it. Even the increase in the consumption of some basic foodstuffs can be explained in the
same way, for a rise in the consumption of such necessities as rice, meat, and even wheat, could serve the same
social function for lower-income rural households that
consumer durables serve for the urban population.

Social mobility could also shed some light on the preference among the rising segments of the population for
certain channels of investment. One obvious example is
investment in residential buildings, where the replace-

ment of mud-brick dwellings by red-brick housing is the main symbol of social advancement in the village, and goes hand in hand with the need for the new type of house to have access to electricity to accommodate the newly acquired consumer durables. Another is the investment of the returning rural migrant in a taxi, minibus, or truck, or any other small commercial enterprise that caters to the desires of the newly rising classes. More generally, for those social groups who have only recently had access to surplus income, investment in industry or agriculture may seem too risky, requiring more capital, a longer gestation period, and greater experience than is required by investment in residential buildings, transportation, tourism, or the import trade. Much of what is regarded by economists as 'unproductive' investment is in the channels preferred by these investors with less experience who are also more anxious to prove their social advancement and less confident in their ability to maintain their newly acquired social status.

I believe it is important to emphasize the relationship between the new patterns of consumption and investment and the rise in the rate of social mobility for at least two reasons. First, it should warn us against exaggerating the ease with which certain types of consumption and investment could be restricted. Critics of the open-door policies often suggest restricting the import and therefore the consumption of popular consumer durables as a way of dealing with some of Egypt's social and economic problems. These restrictions could be more easily enforced had such consumption not been the result of powerful motives and aspirations associated with changes in the social structure. Thus, no degree of improvement in the public transportation system, for example, will be sufficient to dispense with the desire to acquire a private car when such an acquisition serves a purpose so much more powerful than mere transportation from one place to another. On the other hand, the same observation should make us somewhat less pessimistic about the possible continuation of the same patterns of consumption and investment into the distant future. If it is true that the emergence of these new patterns is largely the result of rapid social mobility, one may very well expect them to give way to other more socially desirable patterns as the social structure becomes more stable. In other words, one may expect that as the present social turmoil starts to subside and as the rising classes gain greater confidence in their new social positions, less expenditure may be directed to lavish consumption, and investment expenditure may start to flow into more productive channels.

The acceleration of the rate of social mobility may also shed some light on the problem of the growing deficit in the state budget. Complaints about the tax system in Egypt usually refer less to the low level of tax rates than to the high rate of tax evasion. Tax evasion is, in its turn, blamed on the decline in moral standards and the weakening of loyalty to the state. But this very weakening of loyalty may indeed be seen as partly the result of the change in social structure and in the relative social status of tax payers, tax legislators, and tax collectors. One may argue that there is a big difference between the attitude

to the state of the old class of big landowners and indus-
trialists, who constituted the main tax payers in pre-revolution Egypt, and that of the new classes who made their
fortune in the 1970s and 1980s whether from migration,
trade, real estate and land speculation, or from being connected in one way or another with foreign sources of
income. One would indeed expect the former classes to
have a stronger sense of loyalty and to feel more indebt-
ed to the state which had provided them with the necessary infrastructure in irrigation and drainage projects and
had enforced the law and order necessary for the protection of their interests. In contrast, much of the new
income and wealth accumulated in the 1970s and 1980s
may be attributed not to state activities, but rather to its
inactivity, to the merely passive role of the state in allowing people to migrate, and to its failure to regulate the
rate of inflation and the pattern of investment. If readiness to pay one's taxes has any relationship to the sense
of indebtedness to the state, the newly rising classes in
Egypt would be expected to show a much higher propensity to evade taxation than did the older classes of taxpayers whose income came from agriculture and industry.
After the 1970s, the same weakening in the sense of loyalty to the state could also be expected from members of
the legislative councils who came increasingly from this
same class of *nouveaux riches*, and who had no interest
in patching up loopholes in the tax laws. It is quite possible that the attitude toward the payment of taxes of
someone whose taxable income is relatively recent, unreliable, and irregular, and whose newly acquired income

has served to raise him or her to a higher social class, would be very different from the attitude of one whose source of income is long established and more secure, and whose social standing would not be significantly changed by an increase in income or wealth. While to the latter, the payment of taxes may be like dispensing with some extraneous fat from the body, to the former it may seem like giving away part of the flesh. But, in periods of rapid social mobility, the propensity to evade taxes may be just as strong in the downwardly mobile segments of the population, who have every reason to resist an additional sacrifice that would only hasten their decline, especially as they see their new rivals whom they regard as unworthy of their new wealth, unwilling to accept a similar sacrifice. To these declining classes belongs a good proportion of tax collectors. Their worsening social status makes them more amenable to the acceptance of gifts and bribes, while self-confidence has been undermined by the developing aggressiveness of the rising classes whose increasing defiance of the law seems to meet with the compliance and protection of the state itself.

I have already referred to the rise in the rate of inflation as one of the accelerators of social mobility, but it is also true that rapid social mobility may be a cause of greater inflation. For, insofar as rapid social mobility makes people consume more and strengthens their tendency to invest in channels with a faster turnover of capital, it will raise the level of expenditure which in turn tends to raise the rate of inflation.

It is also not difficult to trace many of the other new patterns of social behavior in Egypt to the rise in the rate of social mobility, so that much of what is commonly referred to as an increase in corruption, lack of discipline, and the spread of consumerism and materialistic values, could be little more than the reflection of an excessive inclination to capture new opportunities, to adapt to new circumstances or to avoid a rapid decline in social status. While the opening up of new opportunities for rapid social advancement whets the appetite of the newly rising classes, the threat of social decline weakens the resistance of the declining classes to all sorts of temptations. In these circumstances, to stick to one's principles and moral standards may well feel more and more like a luxury, while a new system of values attaches greater premium to flexibility, to the ability to exploit new opportunities and to develop connections with those who really matter. Patterns of behavior that were highly regarded in a more stable society such as sticking to one's word or promise, pride and personal integrity, are now less prized. Such values are less fit for a rapidly changing society where loyalty to old relationships, be they friends, spouses, places, or principles appears as nothing more than an excessive sentimentality unbecoming in one who is on the make. The increase in the rate of certain types of crime and the emergence of new ones may indeed be no more than extreme manifestations of these tendencies. The collapse of newly built apartment buildings only a few months after their completion, the repeated encroachment on state-owned land, and the widespread bribing of government officials may be only the symptoms of excessive social ambition or of excessive fear of social decline on the part of individuals who are merely more impatient or defiant than the rest.

During periods of rapid social mobility, family ties tend also to weaken. Marriages may have taken place under circumstances which didn't present the opportunities that are now available to the husband or the wife. Social mobility may also require a physical dislocation which threatens old ties, and an increase in the earning capacity of one of the two parties may create a new feeling of superiority which disturbs the old harmony.

Social mobility may well lead to the marriage of a couple who have achieved the same level of education and have similar earning capacities but who have come from very different social origins, which latter could ultimately bring out differences that were only thinly disguised. Children may also come across opportunities for material gain and social advancement that were not available to their parents, threatening the respect they would once have felt toward their parents and encouraging them to dissociate themselves from their old environment. A father whose real income has been greatly reduced by inflation may also find it difficult to retain his traditional authority over his children, and lose self-confidence with the decline in his ability to meet their demands. At the other end of the scale, among newly wealthy parents, a growing permissiveness in the treatment of children may emerge, with an excessive readiness to comply with their demands. In such a case, children can fulfill a function similar to that fulfilled by consumer goods, with their ability to display the new wealth and to have access to new sources of pleasure which the parents may find hard to enjoy. Indeed, it is much harder for such parents to hide the traces of their poorer origins than it is for their children, with their greater access to modern education, foreign languages, and a natural ease with the consumption habits that their parents have had to learn. For declining families, a similar tendency to show greater leniency toward their children may originate from their anxiety to protect them from a decline from which they have just begun to suffer.

In a book originally published in 1927, a prominent sociologist[3] presented an interesting thesis which may throw important light on a number of other changes in social behavior that have emerged in Egypt over the last three decades. According to Sorokin, in situations where the social structure is relatively stable, the lower classes tend to imitate those patterns of behavior which are associated with the higher classes, but the opposite seems to occur in periods of rapid social mobility, when the declining classes are inclined to adopt many of the values and behavior patterns associated with the lower, but rising, social groups. There are very good reasons to believe this to be true. First, there is the increasing self-confidence acquired by the rising classes resulting from their economic success and allowing them a greater degree of self-assertion. Secondly, there is their sheer spread throughout society, again resulting from their greater income, making their presence much more strongly felt in schools, universities, clubs, and other public places which have previously been the protected domains of the higher classes. Thirdly, greater access to education has led to an increasing infiltration by these rising classes into the media, allowing them greater opportunity for spreading their habits of thought and patterns of behavior to the whole society. Exactly the opposite becomes the fate of the downwardly mobile classes whose influence gradually recedes with the decline of their self-confidence *vis-à-vis* their new rivals and their gradual withdrawal from public life. Willingly or unwillingly, but often unconsciously, they come to accept and even to adopt the new patterns of behavior, and even the moral values, of the lower but rising classes, and to discard their own.

Thus, the age-old contempt for manual labor, which has been associated with low income and low social status, gradually disappears with the success of an increasing number of manual laborers in raising their income and the level of education of their children, and with the increase in the number of young people who have traditionally belonged to the higher income groups and who have now come to accept performing manual labor through sheer economic necessity. Eating and dressing habits, which have always been associated with rural or low-income urban dwellers, have begun to be adopted by higher-income groups, together with a return to old-fashioned ways of furnishing the home, a new appreciation of traditional Arabic music, and the discarding of the habit of giving western or Turkish names to children, in favor of authentic Egyptian or old Arabic names which used to betray more humble origins. The recent and amazing spread of the rural habit of men embracing each other in greeting, even if they have just parted, may be explained in the same way. It is not even far-fetched to see a connection between this adoption of rural and lower-class values and the so-called resurgence of religious movements and the 'Islamic revival.' For what is involved here is not a strengthening of religious belief as much as the increasing observance of religious rituals and ceremonies, and the stricter adherence to an outward pattern of behavior associated with Islam, such as the adoption of the veil by larger numbers of women, the spreading of the custom of starting letters and speeches by invoking 'the name of God, the Merciful and Compassionate,' the broadcasting of the Friday prayer through loudspeakers, and the widespread trend of interrupting the day's work for the observance of the daily prayers on time. The fact that current interpretations of Islam, widely accepted today by Egyptian university students and by the new leaders of religious groups in Egypt, seem less rational and less sophisticated than those prevailing in the early decades of this century, has led some writers to complain of a general decline in Egypt's cultural life. What may be closer to the truth is that a major change has occurred in Egypt's social structure, whereby leaders of the Islamic movement no longer belong to a narrow circle of a highly educated elite, speaking to a small number of urban dwellers. What we are now witnessing is a mass movement of which both the members and the leaders belong to social classes of more humble origin, far less well educated and with much stronger roots in the rural sector.

Social mobility has also had an impact on current lin-
guistic expression as well as on the content of popular
culture. The younger generation now use words and
expressions that were not in use thirty or forty years ago
except by the rural population and lower income urban
dwellers, while the president of Egypt came to be referred
to as the '*rayis,*' a word previously used mainly to refer to
a craftsman. Long, elaborate, and often sophisticated
songs have given way to much shorter songs with slighter
tunes and easier words. In the cinema, television, and
theater, traditional plots, which had for long dominated
films and plays, are giving way to plots in which poverty is no longer associated with honesty and wealth with
vice, or in which access to wealth is no longer confined
to the very unlikely coincidence of a rich man falling in
love with a poor girl or a poor man suddenly discovering
a hidden and forgotten treasure. The most popular of the
new films and plays now treat the access to wealth as an
entirely possible and normal occurrence, but often make
fun of the customs, styles of life, and manners of expression of the older and declining upper classes.[4]

The list of economic and social phenomena that have
emerged or gained in strength in Egypt during the last
three or four decades, and which seem to have strong
connections with the rise in social mobility, is almost
endless. In the following chapters I will treat some of
them, starting with the growth of 'religious fanaticism'
and the growing 'westernization' of society, two phenomena which ironically grew hand in hand and which may
very well have stemmed from the same source. Even in

the final two chapters, which deal with subjects that may appear to be of a very different nature, namely the rise of a 'market culture' and the changing orientation of Egyptian economists over the last forty years, the reader will, nevertheless, note my emphasis on the strong influence of the change in social structure.

2

Religious Fanaticism

In trying to justify his 'socialist' measures of the 1960s, the late Egyptian president, Gamal Abd al-Nasser frequently described Egyptian society on the eve of the 1952 revolution as "the half percent society," meaning that the proportion of the Egyptian population that controlled most of Egypt's resources as well as its political life did not exceed that tiny percentage. This may have been an exaggeration but if so, only a slight one. The statement also hinted at a very small middle class and its relatively weak economic and political position.

Some idea of the smallness and weakness of the Egyptian middle class in the early 1950s can be obtained from a 1955 estimate contained in a British government report on income distribution in Egypt. According to this estimate, 1 percent of the total Egyptian population had an annual income per family of more than LE1,500, compared with less than LE240 for 80 percent of the population. The remaining 19 percent of the population, constituting the 'middle class,' had, therefore, an annual income ranging between LE240 and 1,500 per family.[5] Out of the total population of Egypt in 1952 of 21.4 million, about 200,000 persons could therefore be regarded as constituting the 'higher class,' four million as constituting the 'middle class,' and more than 17 million as belonging to the 'lower class.' This is not inconsistent with what we know about the distribution of agricultural landownership in Egypt in 1952, when about 2,000 families owned about one-fifth of all agricultural land and about two million families (or about half the Egyptian population) owned fewer than two *feddans* per family.[6]

One obviously cannot classify Egyptian society today into 'higher,' 'middle,' and 'lower' classes using the same criteria that were used forty years ago. Land ownership can no longer be regarded as the decisive factor it was then, since other sources of large incomes have become more important. Higher education is also no longer a significant feature of those belonging to the middle class, since several new sources of high income do not require high educational achievement. With the advanced degree of social mobility that has characterized the last forty years, affiliation to certain families is no longer a necessary or sufficient condition for belonging to the 'higher' social strata. 'Westernization,' or the ability to adopt western patterns of behavior, has also lost much of its importance in distinguishing one social class from another as a result of the spread of these patterns of behavior among the lower classes, as well as the rise in social status of sections of the population that have relatively little contact with the West. While income and wealth continue to be important criteria for classifying the population into the three social classes, the nature and the source of income and wealth have lost much of their relative importance in this classification by comparison with forty years ago.

If we take data contained in the 1986 population census showing various estimates of the proportion of the Egyptian population falling under the poverty line, and indicators of income distribution revealed by recent Family Budget Surveys, we may tentatively suggest a level of income of LE300 per month per family in 1990 as the borderline between the 'lower' and 'middle' classes, and of LE10,000 as the borderline between the 'middle' and 'higher' classes. According to this classification, about 53 percent (or 30 million people) of the total population of 56 million would belong to the 'lower class,' about 45 percent (or 25 million people) to the 'middle class', and the remaining 2–3 percent (1–2 million persons) would constitute the 'higher class.'

The two figures on the next page illustrate the change that has occurred in the relative sizes of the three classes over the last forty years. On the left, the ratios between the three classes, based on the data for 1952 referred to above, are 1:20:85, while the ratios for 1990 illustrated on the right are 1:17:20. According to these two classifications, the middle class has increased more than six times in the last forty years while the lower class has grown by only 75 percent, and the higher class five to ten times.

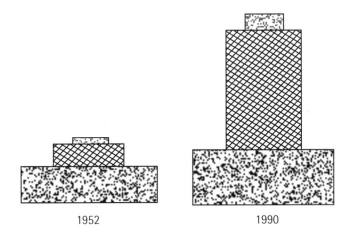

1952   1990

Ratios of the social classes

But no less important than the change in relative size has been the change in the characteristics of the three classes. The new higher class does not consist mainly of the descendants of the older higher classes, but rather of families of recently acquired wealth, whose fortunes were accumulated during the 1970s and 1980s, since such an accumulation of wealth would have been a rarity before the launching of the open-door policies.

The main sources of the new wealth were trade, particularly the import trade, contracting, speculation in land, and commissions. 'Intermediary activities' of all kinds were thus the major source of newly acquired wealth and income, in contrast to the main source of income for the older higher class, namely, the ownership of agricultural land. Like the older middle class, the new middle class includes professionals, merchants, the higher and middle echelons of government officials, owners of middle-sized and small manufacturing firms, holders of middle-sized farms, and owners of urban property. In addition, however, the new middle class also includes some elements of the descendants of the older 'higher class' who have fallen in relative status as a result of the various measures taken by the revolution such as the confiscation of property, nationalization, sequestration, etc. But most importantly, the new middle class now includes, in contrast to the old middle class, a good proportion of craftsmen and of the higher echelons of employees in private and public sector industry. The lower class now includes, as in the past, landless farmers, smallholders, low-income craftsmen, petty traders, and most agricultural and industrial labor, but it now also comprises a good proportion of the lower echelons of government and public sector employees.

Needless to say, the average income of all three classes is significantly higher today than it was forty years ago. The lower class is living, on the whole, much better than the lower class pre-1952, particularly where the condition of health and level of nutrition are concerned, while the other two classes are also enjoying much higher incomes than they did in the early 1950s. This does not necessarily mean that the lower or middle classes are less frustrated or more satisfied with their lot than in pre-revolution days. On the contrary, in view of the unprecedented rate of social mobility of the last forty years, the opposite seems to be the case.

A good proportion of Egypt's 'new middle class,'—surely more than 50 percent and perhaps as much as 75 percent—consists of what may be classed as the 'lower middle class,' where the monthly income per family does not exceed LE600. This lower middle class includes the great majority of the low and middle ranks of employees in government and industrial enterprises, the majority of public sector workers and retail traders as well as a good proportion of those working in private-sector manufacturing firms and small agricultural landholders. There are good reasons to believe that a large proportion of these people has been suffering over the last three decades from growing frustration, dissatisfaction with their lives, loss of self-respect, and feeling that society owes them more than what they are getting. The symptoms are numerous, and are witnessed in the increasing rate of certain types of crime, including crimes against close relatives, a rise in the number of emigrants and of applications to emigrate, increasing corruption at various levels of government, more family break-ups and so on, many of these signs being recorded and reported more by the press and in works of fiction than by social research.

Possible explanations for this increasing frustration are numerous, and most of them bound up with the rising rate of social mobility. The sudden increase in opportunities for augmenting income and accumulating new wealth have whetted the appetite of a large section of the population but caused great frustration among those who, for one reason or another, failed to benefit from them. When the economy started to slacken in the early 1980s, accompanied by the fall in oil prices and the resulting decline in work opportunities in the Gulf, many of the aspirations built up in the 1970s were suddenly seen to be unrealistic and intense feelings of frustration followed. The increase in the rate of unemployment during the second half of the 1980s, reaching, according to some estimates, 20 percent of the labor force (an unusually high rate for Egypt) and considerably higher rates among university and intermediate college graduates, must have intensified this feeling of disappointment in a large section of the population that had pinned great hopes on their own and their children's educational achievements as a channel for social advancement.

All this may bring us closer to understanding the growth of religious fanaticism. A natural tendency toward the stricter observance of religious teachings in the rising sections of the population with very modest social backgrounds, can easily turn into religious fanaticism if associated with severe frustration of earlier hopes of social advancement. It is striking how rare it is to find examples of religious fanaticism among either the higher or the very lowest social strata of the Egyptian population. While members of the higher classes are exempt from the feelings of inferiority experienced by the aspiring lower middle classes, members of the lowest social strata are saved from this frustration by their realization of the near impossibility of changing their relative social position. It is also interesting to note an apparently greater degree of social hypocrisy in the lower middle classes, which could have the same origins, namely, the frustration of unfulfilled ambitions.

Both recent research and studies of earlier parallel experiences in Egypt as well as in other countries, tend to support this conclusion. In his pioneer study of militant religious movements in Egypt, Saad Eddin Ibrahim[7] found that of the thirty-four militants studied who had participated in the attack on the Military Academy in 1974 or belonged to the militant religious group named al-Takfir wa-l-higra, twenty-one, or about two-thirds, were sons of government employees, mostly in middle grades of the civil service, four were sons of small merchants, three were sons of small farmers (owning or holding between six and eleven acres) and two had working-class fathers. With regard to educational level, nineteen of the fathers had intermediate education and only seven had university degrees. According to Ibrahim, "it is safe to conclude that the class affiliation of these militant Islamic groups is middle and lower class. It is also clear from the results of this study that the educational and occupational attainments of most of the members of these groups were decidedly higher than those of their parents,"[8] which indicates an upwardly mobile social stratum that may easily consider its actual attainments to be considerably less than they had originally hoped for or than they deserve.

38

Tackling a much earlier period of Egyptian history, Albert Hourani reached similar conclusions in connection with the growth of the Muslim Brothers' movement in the late 1930s, pointing out that it was "spreading in the urban population among those in an intermediate position: craftsmen, small tradesmen, teachers, and professional men who stood outside the charmed circle of the dominant elite."[9]

Not only failure, however, but success could also be a source of religious fanaticism. Just as this fanaticism could provide an escape from the frustration created by the failure to realize one's material ambitions, it could also provide a useful cover for an accumulation of wealth or income that is either illegal or immoral. Following the 1973–74 rise in oil prices, Egypt witnessed a period of unprecedented increase in income. Between 1973 and 1984, the average annual rate of growth of Gross Domestic Product was 8.5 percent, which was surpassed by very few countries, and real per capita income almost doubled. But very little of this increase in income was attributable to the growth of commodity sectors outside oil. Agriculture was growing at a rate well below that of population growth, and manufacturing at a much slower rate than services and crude petroleum. The major contributors to this rapid growth of income were oil revenues, labor remittances, the Suez Canal, tourism, and foreign aid. The structure of employment showed a similar imbalance in favor of the service sectors. During the period of most rapid growth, from 1977 to 1984, employment in agriculture increased by no more than 9 percent, employment in manufacturing and mining by 38 percent, and in all commodity sectors by 20 percent compared with an increase in services of 45 percent. Egyptian economists have long been warning against the economic dangers of excessive dependence on unreliable sources of income and employment that are subject to factors largely outside Egypt's control, less amenable to policy manipulation, and more sensitive to political fluctuations. There are also good reasons to believe that there may be a strong relationship between the growth of incomes that have the nature of economic rent (i.e., incomes that are 'unearned,' being due more to growth in demand than to greater effort) and the growth of religious fanaticism.

The growth of unproductive activities, and of some incomes that are largely dissociated from effort, seem to provide fertile ground for the growth of irrational habits of thought. Income and wealth that grow at unprecedented rates are more likely to be explained by 'God's blessing' than regular and slow improvements that can be more easily traced to one's own productive effort. Productive activities allow much less leisure for the idle speculation of religious fanatics. Religious fanaticism could also be an alternative source of self-esteem no longer provided by the productivity or usefulness of one's work. But most important of all seems to be the use of religiosity as a cover for illegal, immoral, or undeserved income and wealth. Not only may religious pretense create the impression of deservedness but it could also be a very effective smoke screen to hide forbidden or socially unacceptable behavior. The larger the undeserved commission, or the bribe, or the monopoly price charged to the consumer, or the divergence from the safety requirements of building a block of flats, or from the legal requirements of obtaining an import license, or of benefiting from government subsidies, the greater the degree of pretense of being a good Muslim. Some writers have suggested that the fact that so many Egyptians have spent some years during the 1970s and 1980s in the Gulf countries, where religious tenets are more strictly observed, may have contributed to the growth of religious fanaticism in Egypt. It seems likely, however, that such copying of other people's patterns of behavior cannot become so widespread unless there is sufficiently fertile soil for its proliferation, and what is suggested here is that such a soil has been provided by the unproductive, rentier nature of the Egyptian economy during the last three decades. The fact that the decade of the 1960s witnessed much less religious fanaticism but also fewer symptoms of a rentier economy, may not be sheer coincidence.[10]

The relationship between the growth of a 'rentier economy' and the growth of religious fanaticism in Egypt may be best illustrated by the emergence and growth of the so-called 'Islamic Investment Companies' during the 1980s. These companies managed to mobilize billions of dollars of the savings of Egyptians from their earnings in the oil countries, and competed very successfully with commercial banks in mobilizing labor remittances, by offering considerably higher interest rates (often double those offered by the banking system) and by calling the interest 'profit' to comply with the popular interpretation of Islamic principles. Apart from appealing to religious sentiments and offering a higher financial return, this phenomenon could also be seen as a fascinating example of the impact of a high rate of social mobility on economic behavior. Certain features of these companies and of the way they operated seem to fit curiously well with certain features of the savings invested in them and the nature of the activities and aspirations of those who realized those savings. Having made a big jump up the social ladder through migration to the oil-rich countries, or having achieved other windfall increases in income and wealth, and anxious not to lose their newly acquired social status, investors in those companies found the high return on investment, even though of dubious origin, irresistibly attractive. When the sources of the newly acquired income and wealth were themselves morally suspect, such as currency speculation or obtaining unfair advantage through bribery or other corrupt practices, the secrecy provided by the Islamic Investment companies was particularly welcome, as was, one may add, the religious cover-up provided by them. When the increase in one's income or wealth is of dubious origin, one may be quite satisfied with an explanation of the profit realized and distributed by these companies, as being 'God's blessing,' as these companies actually maintained.

But rapid social mobility, growing frustration among social groups with unfulfilled ambitions, or the growth of a rentier class whose increasing income and wealth are largely divorced from effort, could only account for some of the factors that contributed to the growth of religious fanaticism. Other factors must be involved and could be important, including possible external influences with or without material support. But whatever the role of the external influences, they would probably not have borne fruit had the domestic social and economic environment not made a good part of the population so receptive.

3

Westernization

One of the failings that all post-revolution Egyptian governments have shared is their lack of an original vision of how Egypt's cultural revival would develop. In spite of all the proclamations of the revolution that it aimed at freeing Egypt from colonialism, that it was leading the struggle of the Arab nation for independence, preserving national sovereignty and regaining control of the nation's destiny, and even in spite of the real successes it achieved with regard to certain kinds of 'liberation,' the leaders of the revolution could not rid themselves of the western conception of 'progress.' No one can deny that the Egyptian leaders of the 1950s were sincere in their demand for political and economic independence. Nor would I deny that they achieved a high degree of success in these two fields. But the goal of independence remained confined to these domains alone, and did not extend to other aspects of Egyptian social and cultural life. In fact, any attempt that may have been made in this respect before 1952, suffered a setback at the hands of the July revolution.

Before 1952, the proponents of reform in Egypt had understood it in a wide sense that covered all aspects of social and cultural life. The issue of what attitude to take toward 'westernization' was far from having been resolved; the debate was still raging between the advocates of adopting the western model and those who argued for a return to 'roots,' and for a search for inspiration in Egypt's own cultural heritage, with or without a reconciliation of that heritage with the requirements of modernity. The revolution seemed to have already made up its mind on what path to take, and that was undoubtedly the Western path. It did not, of course, follow the extreme course taken by Atatürk in Turkey, but it did throw all its weight behind the process of westernization, and it took all the steps necessary to tip the balance in its favor.

Thus, however ambitious Nasser may have been, he was not so ambitious as to imagine that the Arabs could develop their own version of 'progress.' His aim was to be equal with the West, but not necessarily different from it. In spite of his great enthusiasm for building more schools and raising the general level of education, no serious question seems to have passed through his mind about the content of this education. He must indeed have worried sometimes about how efficiently it was being carried out, but not about its relation to his own people's cultural heritage and tradition. It was important for the revolution to build new factories, but no serious questions were entertained concerning the justification for producing private motor cars or air-conditioning units, either then or in the future. There was not even any serious debate about the choice of appropriate technology in the new industries that were being established, nor their contribution toward the creation of new employment opportunities. It was considered important to graduate a large number of engineers, but not to spend time choosing a kind of architecture that would be in harmony with the country's architectural and social traditions or with the environment. It was important to wipe out illiteracy, although even in this area there was very little improvement, but it was not deemed that important to protect the Arabic language from further deterioration and neglect. It was important to Egyptianize foreign schools and to bring them under the control of the revolutionary government, but once this was done the teaching of the Arabic language, Arabic literature, as well as national and Islamic history was allowed to deteriorate. For the goal was 'development,' not creativity or innovation.

Perhaps the clearest illustration of this was what Nasser did to the highly respected and prestigious educational and religious institution of al-Azhar. For whatever may be said about the stagnation that had afflicted this institution for centuries and its failure to keep pace with the times, al-Azhar always had, and retains to this day, great potential for devising a new type of education which differs in important ways from the Western model, with respect to both content and methods of instruction. The revolutionary government, however, was of the opinion that al-Azhar could best be developed by being transformed into a replica of the modern national universities. Thus modern subjects like medicine, agriculture and economics were added to the curriculum and taught in foreign languages side by side with the teaching of Islamic law, theology, and classical Arabic, and the management of al-Azhar's colleges was put into the hands of deans who had PhDs from western universities. In this fashion, this great institution was transformed, or very nearly so, into a miserable copy of the existing state universities. Instead of graduating students who were proud of their heritage but able to reinterpret it in the light of contemporary needs, it brought together students who suffered from an inferiority complex because of their inability to reconcile the old religious teachings with the modern sciences.

Although the Egyptian aristocracy prior to 1952, was a class keenly intent on assimilating the western way of life and borrowed the minutest details of its everyday life from the West, it had, in some aspects adhered to tradition more vividly than the new classes which the July revolution had come to serve. This may be explained by the fact that the aristocratic families of the pre-revolutionary days had enough confidence about their place in the world to appreciate that to follow tradition was not always an indicator of 'backwardness'. Thus while it was possible, for instance, for an Egyptian pasha to celebrate the weddings of his sons and daughters with parties including genuinely Egyptian singers such as Umm Kulthum or 'Abd al-Wahab, the *nouveaux riches* of more recent decades have insisted on holding their celebrations at five star hotels to the tunes of western dance music. It was even possible for a powerful Egyptian feudal lord to walk in his fields wearing the *gallabiya* (the traditional dress of the Egyptian peasant) without any feeling of embarrassment, while an Egyptian businessman of today is likely to consider this dress a sign of his humble origins or that he is lagging behind the times. An Egyptian minister in pre-revolution days would have been ashamed to deliver a speech that did not follow the correct rules of Arabic grammar, whereas today we might easily catch a government official being interviewed on Egyptian television dropping in an English word deliberately, and pretending that it was only with difficulty that he could find an Arabic substitute.

When Nasser raised the slogans of 'economic development' in the early years of the revolution, he could not conceive of any meaning for 'development' beyond the narrow meaning that dominated in the West, amounting to little more than raising the rate of growth of GNP. The wider concept of 'reform' or of a 'national revival' as generally understood by Egyptian and Arab reformers before 1952 was now narrowed down to such things as raising the rates of saving and investment, achieving a higher rate of growth of per capita income, increasing school enrollment ratios and the number of hospital beds per 1,000 people, reclaiming new land and building new factories, acquiring new types of armament, and other similar indicators that began to be prominent in the UN annual statistical tables. Nasser's political speeches, like those of other Third World leaders from Cuba to Indonesia, held repeated references to such achievements; they were presented as the main, virtually the only, measure of success or failure of the revolution. Nor was there any significant change after Nasser's conversion to socialism at the beginning of the 1960s. The designation of his socialism as 'Arab Socialism' added hardly anything new to the adopted Marxist concept of socialism which was, as Arnold Toynbee rightly saw it, merely another variety of western civilization. For this 'socialist model' did not depart from the dominant western model except with regard to the issue of equity in the distribution of products; the actual things to be produced remaining essentially the same. Thus, the production of private motorcars was to be continued, albeit with the added goal that many more people should become able to acquire them. Nor was the production of armaments to be discontinued, only its use was now to be in the service of the 'working classes.' While Nasser's socialism raised the slogan of a just distribution of the fruits of development, the fruits of development continued to mean the same thing, namely greater consumption and, more specifically, more consumption of those type of goods and services produced in the West.

Even with regard to 'Arab Nationalism,' Nasser could not conceive of the goal of a 'United Arab State' except in terms of a strong Arab state capable of standing up against western aggression and exploitation, with greater bargaining power, and with Arab oil wealth brought under Arab control, so that the Arabs would be the ones to determine its prices and obtain its full revenues. Some of the more perceptive western commentators on Nasser's policies at that time were fully aware of this; namely that behind Nasser's apparent hostility to the West lay a profound admiration for the western way of life. Such commentators were able to understand the long-term significance of what the Egyptian president was doing to such institutions as al-Azhar, and therefore applauded and gave their full support to the harsh blow dealt to Islamic movements, even though they disagreed with him on almost every other issue.

This trend toward greater westernization, adopted and encouraged by Nasser, increased in strength after his death but also became more vulgar. For while Nasser may have carried a hidden admiration for the West which his political and economic battles did not permit him to express openly, Anwar Sadat left no room for doubt, either in his public statements or in his everyday behavior, about his fascination with western technology and the western style of living. American films were Sadat's daily source of entertainment and European military uniform, the delight of his eye. Whereas Nasser let the foreign correspondents and journalists rely on translations of what he said, Sadat showed himself eager to express himself in English and to show off his knowledge of foreign languages, however imperfect. But perhaps the worst thing about the westernization of the 1970s compared with what went on before was that it constituted mainly the westernization of consumption, while in the 1950s and 1960s it was to a large extent a westernization of production. While in the 1960s Egypt adopted methods of production that were excessively capital intensive, in the 1970s, the country witnessed a very strong trend toward the importing of big cars and innumerable other durable consumer goods. Where the 1960s had witnessed the adoption of a western type of education and the nationalization of foreign schools, the 1970s witnessed increasing laxness in the government's supervision of these schools. It is even possible to view the trend toward a rapprochement with Israel, which characterized the 1970s, as another important step toward increased westernization. For Israel is the product and the ally of western powers. Reconciliation with Israel is essentially reconciliation with the West, and to acknowledge its technological superiority amounts to a new admission of the superiority of the West, while to describe Israelis as 'civilized' and the Arab Gulf states as 'backward,' as Sadat allowed himself to do on some occasions, was a reconfirmation of the belief that Egypt had no choice but to try to walk in the footsteps of the West.

Here may lie one more factor behind the flourishing of some extreme religious movements in Egypt during the 1970s. It is of course true that the greater westernization under Nasser and his harsh treatment of religious fundamentalists must carry part of the responsibility for the growth of these movements after the release of their members from prison in the early 1970s. But the acceleration of westernization during the 1970s surely carries a larger weight of responsibility for the greater violence and fanaticism of these movements. For if it was rapid social mobility that created the fertile soil for religious fanaticism during the last three decades, as argued in the previous chapter, the accelerated drive toward westernization since the 1970s, must have provided this soil with some quick-rooting plants.

How is one to explain this trend toward greater westernization after the 1952 revolution? It is of course possible to attribute it to some character traits in the leaders of the revolution, to their class affiliations or to the inherent admiration in army officers for the technologically advanced weapons of the West. But this probably does not reach the heart of the matter. The process of westernization in Egypt is an old and continuous one that can be traced back to the time of the French campaign of more than two centuries ago. In that sense, the July revolution was only a new link in an already existing chain. But westernization speeded up so much after the revolution because of the speed at which the economic and social change took place at that time. For an economically and socially stagnant society is easily protected, by its very stagnation, from yielding to the invasion of an alien culture, while the rate of change in the invading culture itself must also influence the rate of infiltration into the recipient cultures.

Egypt's history over the past two centuries tends to support this. The degree of westernization of Egyptian society during the eighteenth century was modest, if indeed it existed at all, not only because of the relative stagnation of Egyptian society at that time, but also because Europe had not yet gone through its industrial revolution. The winds of westernization blew over Egypt for the first time with Napoleon's campaign and Muhammad Ali's efforts to industrialize the country and build an efficient army. It increased in intensity during the reign of Ismail, a reign characterized by even more economic and social change in Egypt and coinciding with the acceleration of European colonialism. And while the impulse to westernize during the period between the two world wars continued, it nevertheless slowed down, because of the relative economic stagnation of the 1930s. It became revitalized once more after the end of the Second World War, with the acceleration of Western economic growth and the accelerated efforts at economic development after the 1952 revolution.

It would seem that Egypt is destined always to pay a high price for its rapid economic and social development. For the more Egypt introduces important changes in its economic and social structure and reformulates its social relationships, the more westernization it must swallow. The more income it gains, the more it must lose of its soul.

4

Masters and Servants

One of the best indicators of a rise in the economic welfare of a country is the rise in the economic value of human labor which could be measured by the increase in real wages. A country where human labor can be bought at a price barely sufficient to provide minimum subsistence, is a typically poor and underdeveloped country. But a country where you cannot get hold of a laborer's services unless you provide him or her with a car or two cars for personal use, is almost certainly an economically advanced country. During the fifty years that have elapsed since the Second World War, Egypt has witnessed marked fluctuations in the value of labor, some of which could be attributed to the introduction of certain economic policies, others to purely external factors over which the policy makers have had hardly any control. Rather than showing a smooth rising trend, real wages have gone in cycles characterized by a rise in the price of labor compared with the prices of goods, followed by a rise in the rate of inflation far exceeding the rise in money wages.

What is more surprising, and must be pure coincidence, is that the turning points, whether for the better or for the worse, seem always to occur somewhere near the middle of the decade. A deterioration in the real value of labor seems to have occurred in the mid-1940s, following the end of the Second World War. Then an improvement started to occur in the mid-1950s following the Suez crisis, and a deterioration set in around the mid-1960s, but particularly after the military defeat of 1967. A definite improvement started again in the mid-1970s with the rise in the wave of migration to the Gulf states, but was followed by another deterioration in the mid-1980s with the sudden fall in oil prices and the introduction of the new economic policies of 'economic stabilization' and 'structural adjustment.' It is still too early, at the time of writing, to say whether this deterioration has or has not been reversed. But I think the whole story deserves to be told in some detail.

In the early 1950s a prominent Swedish economist (Ragnar Nurkse) visited Egypt to give a series of lectures at the invitation of the National Bank of Egypt. Some of these lectures dealt with the problem of capital formation in underdeveloped countries, and later became the basis of a famous book with that title. In one of these lectures Nurkse talked about 'disguised unemployment' and said that the highest estimate he had come across for this phenomenon was in Egypt's agricultural sector, where no less than 50 percent of the rural population were estimated to be 'disguisedly unemployed.' Technically, this meant that half of Egypt's rural population could be drawn from working on the land without any noticeable decline in agricultural output, indicating an appallingly low standard of living and productivity. It also implied that a high proportion of the rural population must be willing to migrate to the city, however low the wage rate offered to them there, so long as it was sufficient to cover the cost of minimum subsistence. The actual wage rate at that time was indeed extremely low when compared with the prices of necessities, whether in the city or the village, and the main explanation was that, for the whole of the previous half century, the increase in the rural population far outstripped the increase in cultivated land, while the rate of industrialization was too low for the absorption of a significant portion of the surplus labor.

Things began to change in the mid-1950s with the radical changes in economic policies introduced after the Suez crisis, when much greater efforts were directed toward industrialization and land reclamation. The first phase of the construction of the High Dam was completed during the following ten years, as well as the implementation of the land reform law of 1952. All this led to a rise in the demand for labor considerably higher than the increase in its supply, so that a significant rise in real wages took place in both the rural and urban sectors, along with a very sharp decline in disguised unemployment in agriculture. However, the 1967 defeat was not just the military 'setback,' that official statements liked to call it at the time, but disastrous economically. For about eight years afterward general economic stagnation and a serious decline in the rate of investment resulted in much slower growth in the demand for labor, both in agriculture and in industry, a rise in unemployment and a decline in real wages. Then came the ten years of the 'great exodus' to the oil rich countries from 1975 to 1985, which absorbed a good part of the surplus labor, skilled, unskilled and semiskilled. Many Egyptian families found themselves receiving unprecedently high incomes from their bread winners working abroad, and their bargaining power strengthened in the workplace within Egypt, as migration created a scarcity of labor at home. But after the dramatic fall in oil prices in 1986 came the inevitable decline in demand for Egyptian labor in the oil-producing countries, and the fall in investment rates within Egypt created a fall in real wages and high unemployment figures once more. This was exacerbated by the fall in Egypt's own oil revenues, as well as the introduction of the 'Economic Stabilization and Structural Adjustment' program.

All these ups and downs in the level of employment and in real wages, so easily expressed in numbers, were associated with important changes in aspects of social life that are not so easily measured but no less striking for that. One barometer of these changes is the changing conditions of domestic servants, which are bound to follow the changes in the general conditions of the labor force. When I started to recall the development of the conditions of domestic servants as I have experienced them in my own home from the time of my childhood until today, I was struck to note how much my personal experience confirmed what I had learnt from my readings about the development of the Egyptian economy over the past half century. It is this personal experience which I would like now to relate.

I still remember how, whenever my father and mother felt the need for a domestic servant during the 1940s or the early 1950s, they only had to express this wish to relatives who lived in the countryside, and in no time at all they would be sent exactly what they wanted. So many were those families in the countryside who were prepared to send their sons or daughters to work in the city as domestic servants in return for no more than their bare subsistence of food and clothing. The servants I remember from this period were almost all female, and some of them less than ten years old. They were "more wretched than wretchedness itself," if I may translate my mother's phrase literally. The word 'illiterate' would not convey the extent of their ignorance, for when they arrived in the city they had no inkling of what life in the city could mean and no previous acquaintance of any aspect of city life. On the rare occasion that a motorcar would have passed through their village, people would have come out of their homes to look at it and the young boys and girls might have clapped their hands in admiration. A man (let alone a woman) wearing trousers in the countryside would have seemed like a creature coming from outer space. Television was still unknown anywhere in Egypt, and even the radio was a rare sight in the village, to be heard only in the home of the village mayor. When our little servant girl first looked at our radio, a large one placed high on a shelf where the children could not fool around with it, and heard the voice of the announcer coming out of it, she screamed, "Get out, you lunatic!," as she thought the speaker was hiding inside the radio. The sight of some of those little servant girls in the street carrying the children of their masters was quite astonishing, since one could not easily make out who exactly was carrying whom.

That 80 percent of the Egyptian population which inhabited the Egyptian countryside at the time, was leading a life hardly different from that led by their ancestors in ancient Egypt, whether with regard to their standard of living, the type of goods they consumed or to the methods used in cultivation. Nor could the conditions of domestic servants in the city have been very different from those under the ancient system of 'corvée labor.' For a boy or a girl working in domestic service was often not paid any monetary reward at all, their family residing in the village being content to know that their son or daughter was provided with the necessary food, clothing and shelter which they were hard put to cater for in the village. If the servant was to run away from service and return to his family, it was not difficult to have him returned against his will. A girl servant usually resided full-time in the home of her master, not having a clearly defined job or specific duties to perform; she was permanently on call to carry out the wishes of her employers, whatever they should be. Anything that may be given over and above what was required for subsistence was given as an act of generosity. I remember that my father toward the end of the 1940s, used to give the servant girl (or more precisely to give her father when he came to visit her once every six months or every year) a monthly wage of twenty piasters. If this is to be related to my father's salary, as a university professor at that time, which was about a hundred pounds a month, the ratio between the salaries of servant and master would be 1:500.

On my return from my study abroad in the mid-1960s, I found the conditions of domestic servants radically changed. When we needed a housemaid to help with the housework and in taking care of our little daughter, the maid to be found was no longer a little girl whose parents wanted to get rid of her, but a married woman whose husband worked in a leather-tanning factory, or another whose husband was employed as a waiter in a restaurant, or a third married to a laundryman and so on. The village was no longer the sole nor even the main source of domestic servants for the city, the city itself now capable of generating its own domestic servants. This change was the result of at least two important developments: the greater ability of rural families to provide for their children and the rise in the proportion of working class people in the city, created by increasing industrialization and the growth of all kinds of services. One consequence of all this was that housemaids would now be available for only a few hours every day, after which they would return to their husbands and children. This, in turn, led to a transformation in the relationship between masters and servants. A system which had been close to that of 'corvée labor' had given way to a much more clearly defined system of 'wage labor,' with a specific wage being paid for a specific set of duties. This was the situation in the mid-1960s when my salary as a young university teacher was about forty pounds a month, of which we used to pay two pounds to the housemaid. The ratio between the salary of the servant to that of the master had increased significantly between the mid-1940s and mid-1960s from 1:500 to 1:20.

Between the mid-1960s and the mid-1980s another even greater transformation took place in the Egyptian labor market: labor abundance was succeeded by labor scarcity. The principal cause was the large-scale migration of Egyptian workers to oil-rich countries. People started to complain of the great difficulties they faced in recruiting enough people to work on agricultural land at a 'reasonable' wage, while in the cities people talked about the difficulty of securing the services of all types of craftsmen who were now asking for wages beyond the reach even of a good part of the middle class. I remember how some time in the late 1970s, one of my brothers complained that on calling a plumber to perform a simple job which required no more than half an hour to complete, the plumber quoted forty pounds for doing the work. This sum represented more than a tenth of my brother's salary, even though he was no less than the respected manager of a public sector company. When my brother expressed his surprise and dismay, the plumber replied: "We don't have to do the job now, but you'd better start saving for it from today!"

Toward the end of the 1970s, I returned to Egypt after another long stay abroad. My salary on my return had become more than fifteen times what it had been ten years earlier. But on employing a new housemaid I now had to pay her a much higher proportion of my salary. The ratio of the maid's salary to mine had risen from about 1:20 in the mid-1960s to about 1:15 in 1979. This must have signified not only a narrowing of the gap between the living standards of servants and masters, but also a rise in the ratio between the average income of domestic servants and the prices of some modern household appliances which they never have dreamt of acquiring only a decade earlier. Thus our housemaid, at the beginning of the 1980s, could consider buying an Egyptian-made refrigerator, paying for it in installments, adding, shortly thereafter, a television set and then an electric washing machine. Our housemaid at the time had not just arrived in Cairo from the countryside, as was common in the 1940s and the early 1950s, nor was her husband a factory worker, as had been the case with our maid in the 1960s. Rather, she was the first wife of a man who had left her, with two small children, to marry a divorced woman. He worked as a driver of one of the 'microbuses' which had become a favorite investment for Egyptian workers returning from the Gulf. Remarriage after divorce had also become common among returning migrants, while those countless micro buses were now to be driven at breakneck speed so that they would generate enough income to pay off their installments, in addition to the installments on refrigerators, television sets, washing machines and so on.

But again, the status quo did not last long. With the economic difficulties that started in the mid-1980s a university graduate could no longer be confident of easily finding work in the Gulf and saving enough to be able to marry and buy or pay the key money for a flat. Nor were sufficient numbers of new factories being built to absorb the ever expanding numbers of job seekers, as had been the case in the 1960s, for industrialization had slowed down and become more capital intensive than ever. With the rise in unemployment, the value of labor in relation to the value of goods started on a new decline, and one durable good after another went out of reach. Our housemaid, who has worked for us for twenty years, continues to work for us with the same degree of loyalty and for a much higher wage than she started with, but the ratio of her wage to mine has fallen considerably. Nevertheless, she seems quite satisfied with her lot as she hears of the hardships which her women friends and their unemployed husbands have to face.

5

Public and Private Sectors

When at the beginning of the First World War, more than eighty years ago, my father came to ask for my mother's hand in marriage, one of the merits that recommended him to her family was the fact that he had a '*miri* job,' that is, that he worked for the government. He was a teacher in the Sharia Law School and therefore subject to the governmental rules of appointment, confirmation, promotion and retirement. At that time, these rules assured a government employee a decent life and the highest possible degree of stability and security. No family with a daughter of marriageable age that did not itself belong to the landowning class, could find someone better placed for their daughter's hand than a man who was, in one way or another, affiliated with the government. Thus the popular Egyptian proverb "If you cannot have a *miri* job, wallow in its dust." And there was nothing irrational in this widely held belief at that time.

It was possible to divide Egyptian pre–First World War society into three classes: an upper class representing no more than 1 percent of the population, a lower class that may have exceeded 90 percent of the population, and a middle class of no more than 10 percent. Since the total population of Egypt at that time was about 12 million, it is possible to estimate the lower class at about ten million, the middle class at slightly less than two million and the upper class as an extremely slender stratum at the top whose number may not have exceeded one hundred thousand persons. A large proportion of the middle class consisted of foreigners, who were mainly either owners of agricultural land, traders, or professionals. The proportion of the middle class that derived its income from manufacturing must have been extremely slight. But since the ownership of agricultural land was characterized by a very sharp polarization between a small number of large landowners and a majority of destitute or nearly destitute farmers, the proportion of the middle class that derived its income from agriculture must also have been quite small. So, a good part of the Egyptian middle class at that time derived its income from the government, by working either in education, or in connection with government supervision of agriculture and irrigation, in public health, the police or the army, in the ministries and departments of justice, taxation, and *waqf* (public trusts), in mosques and other religious establishments, or in public transportation and other public utilities.

I do not know of anyone from my father's or my mother's families who, prior to the First World War, received the major part of his income from any source other than the government. No member of either family had been connected with trade or industry, worked in a bank, or was a doctor, lawyer, journalist or in any such profession. There was a teacher and a judge, but they were still government employees. Some of them even owned small plots of agricultural land which yielded modest incomes, but nothing sufficient to provide any of them with a decent standard of living, and so, for all of them, working in the government was their principal source of income.

In spite of all the economic and social changes that Egypt went through during the first half of the twentieth century, the relatively high status of the *miri* job was, at mid-century, essentially the same as it had been before the First World War. Population had of course greatly increased during the forty years separating the First World War and the 1952 revolution, and the middle class had increased, both in absolute number and as a proportion of the total population, because of both the spread of education, which increased the number of professionals, and the growth of industry. Even so, by the mid-1950s, the Egyptian middle class had not yet exceeded 20 percent of the population. And even though the proportion of middle class persons engaged in what Egyptians call the 'free professions' (i.e., *not* employed by the government) such as self-employed doctors, lawyers, engineers, and artists, was greater than before the First World War, nevertheless, government employees continued to constitute a high proportion, perhaps even a majority of the Egyptian middle class at mid-century.

This could be explained partly by the fact that middle class owners of agricultural land had not increased significantly during the first half of the century, and instead the polarization of land ownership between large landowners and holders of very small plots of land or no land at all continued to grow. The growth of industrial output during the interwar period was not associated with a significant increase in industrial employment nor with an increase in the proportion of the population deriving their income from industry. And even though wider education had meant that the proportion of professionals in the total population increased significantly over the first half of the century, most of these were absorbed by the government, either as school teachers, or in the departments of health and justice, or in the administration of public works and other public services and utilities. At mid-century then, the old proverb "If you cannot have a *miri* job, wallow in its dust," was as valid as it had ever been.

The situation of our family at mid-century was a case in point. There were eight children in the family, six boys and two girls, and I was the youngest of them all. Not a single one of my brothers had ever acquired a job other than a government job: two of them became teachers in a state university, the third worked as an engineer in the Ministry of Industry, the fourth in Egypt's Electricity Authority and the fifth in the Egyptian Broadcasting Corporation and later in the Foreign Ministry. I, in my turn, became a teacher in a state university. My two sisters married teachers who also received their incomes from the government. We were all then, in one form or another, 'government employees,' and none of us, as had been the case with my father, ever obtained any significant income from another source. Even though my father was a writer of books and frequently contributed articles to the press for which he was paid, it never occurred to him that these books or articles could one day bring him an income that would provide a reasonable standard of living. The example of Naguib Mahfouz, the internationally renowned author, is another case in point; it didn't occur to him to give up his job in the Ministry of Waqfs, until a very late age, and even then he could not feel completely secure without another job as a regular contributor to a state-owned newspaper.

One of my brothers, who is now over seventy years old, tells me the story of how, on his graduation from the college of engineering, my father flirted with the idea of starting a private business, to establish a new publishing house with its own printing press, and employing this brother of mine as its manager instead of him trying to secure a job in the state-owned Electricity Authority. My father's friends, without exception, were appalled by the idea, and advised him to abandon such a dangerous and risky project which was bound to end by destroying my brother's future. Such a private business, they all thought, was bound to fail and my brother would be greatly grieved, after so many wasted years, to see his fellow graduates having reached the fourth or even the third grade on the government promotion scale, while he would have to start from the bottom of the ladder. My father duly abandoned the idea and remained faithful to the old proverb.

One would be forgiven for thinking that the next two decades, the 1950s and 1960s, witnessed an even deeper entrenching of this conviction, and a stronger attachment to government positions among the middle classes. For those two decades certainly saw an unprecedented expansion in government activities, as a result of wide-spread nationalization and sequestration. There was also a much more active role for the government in opening new schools, universities, factories, and theaters, and an increase in government intervention in almost all walks of life: in agriculture through land reform, in industry and trade through nationalization, planning and various forms of control of new investments, in construction through the requirements of building licenses, in travel and migration through the introduction of the system of exit permits, in cultural life and information, in addition, of course, to the rapid growth of the army and all kinds of services connected with security and intelligence. It seemed in fact that there was nothing left but the *miri*, and what kind of dust was there, other than the dust of the *miri*, to wallow in?

But what was also true was that those two decades were simultaneously preparing the ground for the rapid growth of the private sector. This had started only timidly or secretly in the 1950s and 1960s, but as soon as the doors started to open at the beginning of the 1970s, it gushed out like a flood sweeping away everything in its path.

The two decades following the 1952 revolution had witnessed significant additions to Egyptian society's productive assets. After decades of relative stagnation came considerable increases in cultivated land, industrial enterprises, and all types of construction, all of which were reflected in a rise in the rate of economic growth. Although most of these new productive assets were originally in government hands, once the transformation of the economic system took hold, many of them became privately owned. More importantly, this increase in productive assets created by the state led in turn to the increase in demand for a great variety of activities that by their very nature had to be performed by the private sector, such as lawyers, engineers, accountants, traders, contractors, and intermediaries of all kinds, as well as the services of craftsmen and owners of small means of transportation.

In the long run, though, perhaps the most important contribution of the 1950s and 1960s to the growth of the private sector was that period's contribution to the acceleration of the rate of social mobility. For increasing social mobility encouraged private initiative and stimulated the growth of private enterprise in any area that was not encroached upon by the state. When, in the 1970s, the domination of the state started to decline, the field became wide open for the rapid growth of the private sector.

It was therefore only natural that the belief in the superiority of working a government job should start to go into decline during the 1970s, as examples started to accumulate of the possibility of achieving considerable financial success through a private activity that had nothing to do with the government. This started to appear first in small commercial enterprises, currency trading, real estate, contracting activities, construction, and in leasing furnished accommodation to foreigners or Arab tourists. Then came the general conviction that a considerable improvement in one's standard of living could be achieved by a few years' migration to the Gulf. The sudden rise in the rate of inflation after 1975 also showed how one could augment one's wealth by seizing the opportunity of buying and selling certain goods at the right time, while others during this period started to realize how they could make a fortune merely by exploiting the growing weakness of the government and the public sector, a weakness that showed itself in increased corruption, the decline in the rule of law, and the growth of favoritism.

On the other side, government employees were suffering from the conspicuous deterioration in their status in relation to the examples of success they saw flashing about them in the private sector. While inflation was boosting the coffers of private sector entrepreneurs, it was rapidly destroying the economic and social status of government employees and casting serious doubt on their legendary economic security. The government did indeed continue to guarantee a job for every university graduate, but what sort of a job was it where pay increased with the pace of a turtle while prices soared with the speed of a rocket? It was becoming increasingly clear that "if the *miri* happened to approach your door, then you must try to run away from it with the utmost haste!"[11]

Both trends, the rise of private business and the decline in status of government employees, continued throughout the 1980s and 1990s but with one important difference, namely the gradual improvement in the moral reputation of the private sector. Examples of people gaining riches by immoral means were, and still are common, but many of the cruder and more outrageous examples, such as brand new residential buildings collapsing on the heads of their occupants as a result of the negligence and greed of the original contractors, have disappeared. At the same time, examples of socially responsible private investment genuinely contributing to productive assets and people's welfare were on the increase. The net result of the development of the last thirty years has therefore been, not only the rapid growth of private enterprise at the expense of the government, but also a rise in the reputation of the private sector. 'Good families' are now ready to give their daughters in marriage to young men who do not have secure jobs for life, nor a good pension scheme, but are engaged in a private venture which has a promising, even if somewhat risky future, especially if they show signs of being bright, ambitious, and determined to succeed.

When I now compare my own generation with the generation of my children, I am struck by the change that has occurred in the relative status and people's estimation of government jobs and private business. We were eight brothers and sisters. All the men earned their living from government jobs and the two women had no job outside the home but married government employees. Between us, our children are nineteen in number, three of whom are either still at school or who, having completed their studies, preferred not to work outside the home and to dedicate themselves to bringing up their children. Of the remaining sixteen, nine work in the private sector, one works in a bank jointly owned by the public and private sectors, and three chose permanent migration. Only three work in the government or the public sector, even though one of them recently decided to resign from her government job, content with the modest pension she receives. She had apparently found that the cost of commuting between her home and her office was greater than the difference between the salary and the pension. Thus, in one generation, the proportion of those working for the government from a middle class family has declined from 100 percent to only 16 percent.

Although this development may be startling, it is difficult to describe it as either good or bad. There is hardly any doubt that it indicates an increase in vitality, a higher level of activity, a higher standard of living and greater ambition. But it also implies less stability, greater tension, less leisure time, shorter vacations and less security for the future. Does it also entail greater freedom? I am not at all certain, for one may indeed feel more free with greater prosperity, but is surely less free to the extent that one is more anxious about the future and has less time to exercise this freedom.

6

The Position of Women

When it occurred to me to review the changes that have taken place in the position of women in Egypt over the last fifty years, I decided not to mention anything that I had not seen with my own eyes nor had direct personal experience of. It seemed appropriate to confine myself to a comparison between my mother's way of life as I knew it as a child and young boy, and that of my daughter after she married and had a child of her own. I found it necessary however, to exclude anything untypical in their experiences.

When I start comparing the way my mother lived about fifty years ago and the way of life of my daughter today, I am really astonished by the differences. I also find myself feeling surprised at those who are unwilling to acknowledge the degree of intellectual and psychological emancipation that Egyptian women have achieved. My daughter has a job which occupies her from early morning until late in the afternoon. It is not a routine job but requires initiative and a lot of mental effort. Before she goes to work, and after she returns home, she attends to the requirements of her small child, to running the household, and to the needs of her husband. At the same time, she is working for a postgraduate degree which requires her to attend two evening lectures a week—for which she has to drive through some of the most crowded and nerve-racking streets of Cairo—to prepare for lectures and examinations, and to write research papers. In spite of all these demands, she gives much more attention to her appearance than my mother ever did, she chooses what she wears much more carefully and takes far greater pains to make her home comfortable and elegant.

What was it then, that my mother was doing with all the time that was available to her? My mother never had a job, never worked for an academic degree and did not spend much time on her appearance or in making her home beautiful. She never learnt to drive a car and indeed rarely left her house. She had neither a video nor a television set to watch, nor do I recall ever seeing her putting a record on the gramophone or listening to the radio, and she only rarely went to the cinema or to the theater. She rarely even read beyond a quick glance at the lighter columns of the newspaper. She was not as skillful as my daughter is in choosing the right toys or books for her children, for people did not take such things so seriously at that time, and in any case, she seemed to have neither the time nor the composure to give them much thought. She did not have the time? Why? What on earth was she doing then, if she did none of these things?

Could it be that the kitchen was really all that occupied her? Yes indeed, almost all my mother's time was spent on cooking or on matters connected, in one way or another, with food. But that kitchen, in which she spent most of her time, was nothing but a cramped little place with very poor ventilation, no comfortable place to sit or work and no glimpse of beauty. It was also an extremely hot room in the summer, particularly when the primitive petrol stove was lit. My mother was always either coming from the kitchen or going to it, dripping with sweat as she prepared food for one son after the other as they arrived home from school at various hours of the day. None of us was willing to wait even a quarter of an hour until another brother's return so that one meal could be prepared for both; each demanding his right to eat as soon as he arrived home declaring that he would otherwise die of starvation. She would feel sorry for us and bring us the food, which we royal highnesses would then gobble up without making the slightest effort to exchange a few words with her beyond a critical comment on this or that dish. Then we would run off for a nap, or to go to a session of 'homework' with a group of friends.

My mother would often laughingly repeat the verse "We feed you for the sake of God, expecting neither compensation nor your thanks," and I don't believe she ever thought that there was anything odd about this pattern of life. Even my father, with all his education and liberal-mindedness, did not appear to find anything unusual in the way my mother was treated. In his autobiography, in a description of his feelings and impressions on seeing Europe for the first time, he recorded his thoughts about the possible causes of the advance of European nations over the Muslims and the Arabs, attributing this to two factors, one of them the higher position of women, and the other the abundance of rainfall. If we were to gloss over rainfall, there may indeed be a good measure of truth in the other explanation, but it certainly did not look as if my father made much effort to advance the position of women within his own household. Or perhaps he discovered earlier on in his marriage that no matter how hard he might have tried, he would never have been able, by his efforts alone, to bring about any significant change in the position of women either in his own family or outside it.

My mother represented a whole generation of Egyptian women deprived of any means of earning a living independently from their husbands, and in most cases educated to a level that would not enable them, even in theory, to earn such an income. They were raised to regard men as their source of economic security, but a very unreliable source at that. A woman therefore had to develop skills to retain her man, for if she did not she would be exposed to an unenviable fate. It is no exaggeration to compare the relationship between a husband

and wife in Egypt at the time with a political relationship governed by the arts of war and diplomacy, of cunning and craft, rather than love and friendship.

Like most Egyptian women of her generation, my mother learned from childhood the crucial lesson that a wife must clip her husband's wings if he was not to fly away and that the most effective way of achieving this was to bear him as many children as possible. The inevitable result was that my father, who had planned to have only two children, partly out of a sense of duty toward his overpopulated country and partly to be able to afford a proper education for them, ended by having eight. If a woman was to praise her husband, in my mother's days, she would extol him by declaring that there wasn't a need in the household that went left unprovided for. The best of men was he who was 'liberal of hand,' and the worst was he who spent his money 'outside his household,' whether on drugs, gambling or on other women. A wife in those days would tolerate many things of her husband that an Egyptian wife now would find unforgivable, so long as he spent lavishly on his household.

I do believe that it was my mother's economic dependence on my father that cast the shadow on their life together. It was not a relationship completely lacking in love and affection, but the moments of tenderness came at infrequent intervals, rather like the sun's rays shining through a heavily clouded sky.

How far we are today from all of this! Egyptian women have made great progress in breaking through this economic dependence; they have gone outside the home to earn a living or to get an education. In many fields they have become men's equals, working with them as colleagues in government offices, in private companies, and in universities. With the increase in the rate of inflation and the rise in the cost of living, men have started to value their wives' ability to share the burden of making a living and this has led to a preference for fewer children, smaller homes with a smaller kitchens, and less cooking. A woman's essential functions have therefore been radically changed, and the relationship that once resembled a military or a political relationship is now characterized by greater affection—or at least a greater demonstration of it—and more mutual respect. The chief quality in a husband no longer resides wholly in 'his pocket,' as my mother used to say, but, in other things that have little to do with economics.

This may shed some light on why the sort of love songs that used to stir the hearts of my mother and father are so different from those that move my daughter and other women of her generation. One may indeed marvel at the amount of tears that singers of my parents' generation used to shed. They sobbed over the great distances, real or imaginary, that separated them from their beloved and the sleepless nights that were spent longing for him or her. Compare this with the *joie de vivre* and the optimistic anticipation of actually meeting the loved one expressed in today's love songs. The sadness that reigned over the love songs of my parents' generation was surely only a reflection of that rigid and virtually complete separation between the sexes and the different universes they inhabited. When my father and mother would shed tears on hearing the old love songs of Umm Kulthum, 'Abd al-Wahab and 'Abd al-Muttalib, they were probably only crying about the love they had never really experienced.

It occurred to me to test the validity of my conclusions about this economic interpretation of the position of Egyptian women by comparing the position of my sisters, and their relationships with their husbands, with those of my mother and my daughter. My findings appeared to support my earlier conclusion, for my sisters seemed to occupy a middle position between my mother and my daughter both in the degree of their economic dependence and in the nature of their marital relationships. While my sisters were more independent economically than my mother, they were also treated with much more respect and tenderness by their husbands. Neither of my sisters ever had a job outside the home, nor did either earn an income through her work, but the extent of their education allowed at least for the possibility that they could do so if need arose. Opportunities of work for middle class women had opened up a little between my mother's and my sister's generations but of course had multiplied several times by the time my daughter finished her education.

If what I have suggested is at all close to the truth, then one should think twice before regarding the spread of *hijab*, which middle class women tend to use nowadays to cover their hair, as a setback in the process of women's liberation in Egypt. Over the past fifty years, Egyptian women have achieved remarkable progress in their relationships with men, in their intellectual emancipation , in their self confidence, and in their ability to speak out. Just as the wearing of the *hijab* is not an unquestionable proof of a woman's virtue, it is not an indication of narrow-mindedness or fanaticism, as many people seem to think. The spread of the *hijab* represents a trend toward greater movement of previously secluded women into the outside world, rather than a confinement. For the adoption of the veil has not taken place among liberated women so much as among women who previously were largely housebound, allowing them to enjoy much greater freedom of movement but with a cover over their hair.

But one should beware of seeing in all this an unequivocal sign of progress on all fronts, for it is far from certain that women of my daughter's generation are in all respects better off than those of my mother's generation. For all their subservient relationship to their men, women of my mother's generation did enjoy a greater degree of stability and less disruption of family life. This was also reflected in their children who, on the whole, seem to have shown much less signs of anxiety and less restlessness than is seen in today's younger generation. So, once more I find myself reaching an ambivalent conclusion about the position in which we find ourselves today. Here again, wider opportunities and greater economic freedom seem to have been obtained at the price of less freedom in other realms of life.

7

The Arabic Language

Anyone who still remembers the respect and esteem with which Egyptians regarded the Arabic language forty or fifty years ago, cannot help but be grieved by the treatment it receives today. People used to take pride in being able to write good Arabic, in being well acquainted with the rules of Arabic grammar and in observing them even in writing an ordinary letter, let alone in giving a speech in public. This was made possible for our generation by the teachers we had, themselves masters of the language. It was taken for granted that a journalist, even if he was only writing a short news report, or a radio announcer, should have a perfect command of Classical

Arabic. When ministers and politicians delivered speeches, they did so in polished Classical Arabic, and one of the standards by which this or that politician was judged was the force of his eloquence and the beauty of his language. The Academy of the Arabic Language, whose members included the masters of literature and learning in Egypt, enjoyed great respect and veneration. It was presided over by Ahmad Lutfi al-Sayid until his death, and later by Taha Husayn. Obtaining membership to the Academy was considered an honor equal to none, and a life's crowning achievement.

All this belongs to the past. To commit a grammatical mistake while writing or giving a speech in Arabic is no longer something to be ashamed of. Indeed the prevailing atmosphere may make one feel pedantic even to be calling attention to such errors. Mastery of Arabic is no longer a condition for broadcasting, and today's journalists are continuously committing lexical and grammatical mistakes. As for ministers and politicians, it is no longer conceivable, with their busy schedules and their frequent interaction with foreigners, to demand that they pay attention to such trivialities. Hardly anyone today can call to mind the names of a few members of the Academy of Arabic Language, and the time when we would hear of a new expression the Academy had coined as an equivalent for a foreign word or term that had begun to be frequently used is long gone. The Academy can no longer keep pace with the flood of foreign terms and expressions that has swept into everyone's use of Arabic.

In fact, far from people deriving pride in good Arabic, the opposite seems to be the case. Several female television announcers, for example, seem to take pride in the fact that they cannot pronounce Arabic words properly, apparently believing that it points either to her overwhelming femininity, or to the fact that she is immersed up to her ears in a foreign milieu. Interlocutors on television or radio programs seem to be quite willing to let foreign words slip into their speech from time to time, pretending that they have done so unconsciously or reluctantly, apparently not being able to find suitable Arabic equivalents for these difficult foreign terms. Writers in newspapers or magazines, even popular ones, just like university professors, seize every opportunity to use the foreign equivalent for an Arabic term, even if the Arabic equivalent is quite appropriate and unambiguous, or even clearer and more precise than its foreign counterpart. Thus an Egyptian economist may write the words 'prosperity' or 'wealth' next to their Arabic equivalents, as if the Arabs had never, in their history had any experience of prosperity or wealth. University textbooks are filled with foreign terms, next to their Arabic equivalents, and often without them, to create the impression that the author is tackling a difficult subject which only those who know the foreign language can comprehend. The number of writers and university professors who appear from their writings not to think in Arabic, but in a foreign language, has increased over the years. This sometimes reaches such extremes that the reader has mentally to be able to translate what he reads in Arabic into the foreign language if it is to become at all intelligible. In such cases understanding something written in Arabic becomes dependent, not on the extent of your knowledge of Arabic vocabulary and grammar, but on the extent of your knowledge of a foreign language and its conventions.

This is truly an unfortunate state of affairs and one may wonder what brought it about. One obvious cause must be the rapid expansion of education, accompanied by a general decline in standards including the standard of language teaching. Another possible factor is the change in the mediums through which knowledge of Arabic is transmitted, for school is no longer the sole medium for such transmission and perhaps not even the main one. Newspapers, magazines, the radio, and partic-ularly, television play a much more important role in set-ting the standard of the language than ever before. And the media are quite distinct from schools and universities in the way that they transmit information. They address the broad masses, whose educational levels are generally inferior to those of school pupils or university students. A mass media writer may thus excuse himself for the scant attention he gives to Arabic grammar under the pretense that his public does not require or comprehend anything better. The undue speed with which journalistic, radio, and television materials are prepared, leads to another excuse that there is insufficient time to attend to gram-mar, and that what is important is the 'content.'

But not even these points adequately explain the pre-sent predicament of the Arabic language. It seems to me that the main source of trouble lies not in a lack of ability, but rather in a lack of will; it is not that people are no longer capable of expressing themselves correctly in Arabic, but that people no longer want to do so, or are no longer willing to make the effort. If this is the case, then it will never be enough to produce competent teachers, or to ensure that quality is not sacrificed to quantity. For the main culprit once again may be the high rate of social mobility.

To explain this, I would like to distinguish three generations of learners in Egypt, with respect to their class affiliation, to their attitudes to the West, as well as to their attitudes to the Arabic language. The first generation, who received their education during the 1930s and 1940s, belonged to a relatively stable social class, felt secure about their social status, and were not haunted by a past which they despised or were anxious to forget. This was reflected in a confident attitude toward cultural tradition and a respect for their own language. Yes, there was a bedazzlement and an enchantment with the West, but this did not presume western superiority in all aspects of life and certainly did not extend to the field of literary production or to the Arabic language. Things started to change radically in the 1950s and the 1960s. As a result of the economic and political measures taken at the time of the revolution, and the profound social transformations these measures gave rise to, including a very rapid expansion in education, the majority of those who were educated in the 1950s and 1960s belonged to a lower class or had recently risen from more humble social origins. They were therefore much less secure about their social status, and aspired to still greater social advancement. The attitude of this class of learners, I maintain, was less reverent toward their national language, and showed much less patience with its rules. If one compares the speeches of the leaders of the 1952 revolution with those of politicians of the pre-revolution years, one would be struck by the extent to which the leaders of the revolution were ready to flout the rules of grammar and polished expression, and permit themselves to deliver speeches in the colloquial language, something that earlier generations of politicians would never permit themselves to do. What seemed important to the new breed of politicians was revolutionary change and for its sake, all 'formalities,' including Classical Arabic grammar, could be readily sacrificed.

Things became even more serious during the 1970s and 1980s. The rate of social mobility went on rising—with the continued expansion of education, the higher rate of inflation and emigration to the oil-rich countries—and this coincided with a period of ever closer contact with the West, reflected both in a great rise in the number of foreigners visiting or residing in Egypt and in the quantity and variety of goods being imported. The rising classes welcomed this change and seemed to enjoy using the new symbols of the good life as a kind of payback for the many years of deprivation that they preferred to forget. But the past they were trying to forget included, among other things, the strict observance of the rules of their own mother tongue. The same period witnessed, of course, a counter movement of closer adherence to tradition, but these apparently contradictory trends are, in my opinion, two sides of the same coin. Both succumbing to and revolting against growing Western influence would seem to be normal reactions of various sections of the population to the same stimulus. In both cases, the changes in social behavior are attributed to changes in psychological attitude. But, just as with other psychological ailments, it is far easier to make the diagnosis than to prescribe the cure.

8

Migration

My father was still a young man when he was appointed a teacher of Arabic at a school in Tanta at the beginning of the 1900s. He and his family lived in Cairo, and he felt extreme apprehension about having to travel to Tanta, a city only 100km from Cairo, and live there by himself. He had never before been on a train; he had never even seen the pyramids of Giza. His only journeys had been from his house to al-Azhar, to take his lessons, and then home again. Many years later, having become a well-known writer, he published an autobiography in which he described his anxiety about the trip to Tanta: "If, at the age of sixteen, as I was when I went to

Tanta, a young man would hear today that he is to travel to Singapore or Tokyo or Malaya, he would not feel the anxiety that I felt about my trip to Tanta. I packed up my belongings, a mattress, pillow, blanket, prayer rug, my clothes, and some books, said goodbye to my family and spent my train journey crying."

Forty years after this great event, my eldest brother received a government scholarship to go to England to study for a doctorate in engineering, he was overcome with joy, as was my father on his behalf. My mother, however, was stricken with grief, for she could not imagine how she could live with her son so far away from her. She tried everything to make him give up the idea, or to influence my father into calling the trip off, but she was unsuccessful. She spent several months, before her son's departure, sobbing and wailing and we would sometimes be woken up in the middle of the night by her crying and screaming while she described the flame that was eating up her heart at the thought of being separated from her son.

There is no reason to doubt the apprehension that Egyptians generally feel about traveling, their aversion to leaving their country and having to live abroad, or the intensity of their longing to return if they do leave. I witnessed all of this when studying in England in the late 1950s, where I was able to compare the attitudes of students of other nationalities and their keenness to meet new people, with the Egyptian students who would seek out each other's company, hardly mixing with strangers.

In the cafeteria of my college in London, I saw how an Egyptian would always take his meal with a group of Egyptians, their loud peals of laughter ringing out as they exchanged jokes in Arabic. Some Egyptian students would arrive in London carrying heavy loads of white cheese or whatever type of food they were accustomed to eating back home, for fear that they might not find something like it in England.

No wonder that emigration has played an insignificant role in Egyptian history when compared with that experienced by, say, Lebanon or Greece. This has remained true even during the harshest periods of Egyptian history. In the middle of the twentieth century, shortly before the 1952 revolution, the great majority of Egyptians were living at a level hardly above subsistence, but this did not lead them to consider searching for a better life outside Egypt. They continued to speak of the great beauty and delights of their country, and to sing songs that counted Egypt's many blessings and to intone with great emotion, Sayyid Darwish's popular song expressing the joy of returning safely to the homeland and stating categorically that "the boat that brings you back is far superior to that which takes you away!"

One reason for the Egyptians' historical aversion to emigration may lie in the vastness of the deserts that surround the Nile Valley; to emigrate would mean to leave that valley and go through barren and terrifying lands that no roads or train traverse. Another explanation is given by Gamal Hamdan, our distinguished geographer: "Navigation across the length of the Mediterranean is helped by the westerly wind which prevails during the winter, and across its width by the northerly wind that blows in the summer. Since these prevailing wind directions, particularly in the days of sailing, encouraged navigation from the northern coast to the south, and from the western basin to the east, more than in the opposite directions, this may partly explain why navigation was directed more toward Egypt than away from it." Hamdan then goes on to describe Egypt as being "in one-sided isolation, i.e., the world does not tire of coming to her... [she is] a zone of entry with no exit... nearly everything comes to her but seldom does she go to anyone. This is true of traders and sailors, of migration and campaigns of conquest, as well as of colonial movements. (Should we also add to the list even the Nile itself, and the winds?)"[12]

What started to happen during the 1970s is therefore particularly astonishing. Emigration had started, albeit rather reticently, in the mid-1960s, but almost all those who emigrated at that time were in the higher echelons of society. They were either educated Egyptians with high qualifications, or capitalists who had been adversely affected by Nasser's nationalization and sequestration measures and by the crumbling of Egypt's class structure in which they had occupied a privileged position. They were mostly heading for Canada or the United States. Starting from the mid-1970s, however, emigration assumed a very different guise, in the type of people who were migrating, where they were migrating to, and the length of time they were abroad. The vast majority of emigrants were now unskilled or semi-skilled and their destinations were the oil-rich countries of the Gulf or Libya. Most of these new migrants were only in temporary migration, and intended to return after the few years deemed necessary to 'establish themselves,' an expression the migrants and their families used often at the time. This meant accumulating enough savings to enable them to lead what they considered to be a decent life in Egypt.

Suddenly, Egyptians were not only ready but even keen to emigrate. So much so, that that out of the total population of forty million, three to four million were living abroad by the late 1970s. Egyptians were now competing with each other for the opportunity to work abroad, and considered such an opportunity as tantamount to a new lease of life. Husbands were willing to leave their wives and children behind for years at a time, and the wife became ready to do the same, while the families left behind accepted and sometimes even rejoiced at the golden opportunity.

How is this sudden change of attitude to be explained? Was it the increasing difficulties encountered in trying to make a living at home? This may have a lot to do with it. But life had not been so very much easier for most people during the preceding decades. Why then this sudden yearning to emigrate?

The change must have something to do with the so-called 'revolution of rising expectations.' The sudden rise in oil revenues and the insatiable demand of the oil-rich countries for the labor of poorer Arab states had suddenly given people a real chance to improve their standard of living. And just as importantly, this had became much

more desirable. Television fed the desire for a higher standard and more modern way of life, and many goods and
services that had been regarded as luxuries were now
seen as necessities. After a few years of intensive emigration, Egyptians who had stayed at home started to talk of
the migrants having brought on their return home *the*
refrigerator, *the* television set, or *the* Japanese fan.
Whether this was said with pride, admiration, or envy,
such goods were always mentioned with the definite arti-
cle, indicating that their acquisition had become the goal
and purpose of the whole exercise, and that life had
become almost inconceivable without them.

Egyptians were also encouraged to emigrate by the
fact that they were going to countries that spoke the
same language as they, as well as by the affordability of
modern transport compared with what was available to
earlier generations. Air travel had become accessible
even to some of the poorest sections of the population. It
became quite common to see a row of Egyptian laborers
boarding a plane to one of the Gulf states, each one trying to push ahead of the others, as if they were boarding
a crowded bus leaving Cairo for a small town in the
Delta. Cairo International Airport, situated at the far eastern side of Cairo, took over the important position previously held by Egypt's main railway station in Bab al-
Hadid, now called Ramses Square. It was now the airport
that brought people together or separated them, where
tears were shed on meeting loved ones and departing
from them, an honor formerly confined to the railway
station. I still remember the awe associated with that sta-

tion when I was a child, and the feeling of joy it aroused in me whenever I accompanied a member of my family to meet a close relation of ours. The railway station today has declined physically as much as it has in status, and both conditions of preeminence have been inherited by Cairo Airport.

If my father spent the whole of his first journey to Tanta sobbing, he admitted to me that he was also fearful when, at the age of fifty, he took the plane to attend a conference in London. As for me, I traveled by airplane for the first time when I was fifteen, and my daughter did it when she was only four months old. Fifty years ago, the only member of my family who was living abroad was my eldest brother, who was then doing his post-graduate studies in England, and even he soon returned and settled down in Egypt. Today I can hardly count the number of people from my family who have left Egypt to live abroad, either in permanent migration to the United States or Australia, or as temporary migrants to the Gulf. And more and more now, when one of these 'temporary migrants' returns to Egypt and we think he is finally home to stay, it turns out that he has not quite 'established himself' and that this might require at least one more visit. It is true that none of these people really intends to settle abroad for ever, for most migrant Egyptians still do it in the manner of Ali Baba. He mounts his donkey and goes to the cave which he knows to contain fantastic treasures. When he calls out "Open sesame!" and the door of the cave opens, he scoops out whatever he can as quickly as possible so that he might return home before he is found out, for he can only really enjoy what he has won if he shares it with his wife and children. But it is also true that Egyptians are no longer as afraid of traveling as they once were, and some may even embark on it with a degree of joy and optimism that was inconceivable fifty years ago. Perhaps Egyptians have also become accustomed to moving faster and traveling lighter. They no longer find it necessary to carry their pillows, mattresses, and prayer rugs with them whenever they go, as my father did when he took the train to Tanta. In any case, much sentimentality that was tolerated on a train is no longer allowed for on an airplane.

9

Private Cars

If we were to imagine a person from another planet landing on one of the streets of downtown Cairo at any hour of the day, what could he possibly think of this thing that we call the private car? Let us suppose that no one had told him anything about it, that for instance, we consider it a quick, convenient, and economical means of transportation; would this occur to him as he saw these thousands of cars parked on both sides of the road, or proceeding at the pace of a turtle through narrow streets, moving forward for a few moments and then stopping again, each one occupied by one person or two when it has space for four or five?

Anyone who knew the streets of Cairo in the 1940s and 1950s, when public transport, including the tramway and the public bus, was the common means of getting from one place to another, must be seized with astonishment at the extent of man's foolishness. Today, the streets are overrun with private cars while public transport has failed to grow to meet the demand. Who could have thought that covering the same distances, in the same streets, with a much greater number of private cars, would be a more rational way of transporting people from one place to another than to use a larger number of buses or trams, metro cars, or train coaches?

One has to admit that the Cairo suburbs and the number of people wishing to come downtown each day, from the suburbs as well as the provinces, has greatly increased. But this should have required that the streets be used more efficiently, which would surely have meant a greater reliance on public transport. The real motive behind this astonishing transformation must therefore have been a very different thing from the facilitation of movement from place to place.

Fifty years ago, the privilege of possessing a private car was confined to an extremely small percentage of the Egyptian population. A car was ordinarily purchased only by a person who, as well as having the means, had passed the age at which he or she could reach the tram or bus station easily. The sight of someone in their twenties or thirties driving a motorcar, to say nothing of a sixteen-year-old boy or girl was rare. Few, except those who sought to make their living as a driver, learned how to drive. When a person reached an age when he needed and could afford a private car, it was usually necessary to employ a private chauffeur.

People were accustomed to using public transport, whether within the city or between Cairo and other cities.The train was the principal means of traveling from Cairo to Alexandria and the other provincial cities. This is how the main train station at Bab al-Hadid, the point you had to reach if you wanted to go from the capital to anywhere in Egypt, came to occupy a position of such importance in the lives of Egyptians. The road network around the country was very limited—it usually ran parallel to the train tracks in any case—while travel in the desert in private motorcars was a risk taken only by eccentrics who fancied exploring the unknown.

During the 1920s and 1930s my family lived in Heliopolis, toward the east of Cairo, while my father worked in Giza, in the far west. But in spite of the distance between the two, he never felt that having a private motorcar was one of life's necessities, and it did not occur to him to purchase one, though he could have afforded it. Our house was near the last tram stop, and also near the stop for the bus, which we used to call by the name of the English company that produced it—Centercroft—as well as the stop for the elegant Metro that covered the distance between Heliopolis and 'Imad al-Din Street in the centre of Cairo in a flash. Inside the Metro, you would regularly encounter the conductor dressed more elegantly than a present-day policeman, while the ticket-inspector looked no less elegant and dignified than today's police officer.

My father did not feel the need to buy a car until he was fifty years old, shortly before the Second World War. Since he did not know how to drive, to say nothing of his extremely weak eyesight, he employed a driver. It was perfectly clear, however, to all members of the family, that the car was his, and was not to be used by anyone else except if he was with them. It never occurred to any of my brothers or sisters, even after they had grown up, graduated, and started working, that they could get around any other way than by public transport.

In the 1940s my family moved to live in the district of el-Dokki, to be nearer to the university in Giza, but I still remember that throughout the 1940s and 1950s, the bus remained an easy and convenient means of transport. I used to walk to and from my secondary school, which took me about half an hour each way, and my brothers did the same to get to university. My father would have regarded going to school or college by car as the ultimate in pampering and impudence. One of my brothers tells me that during the whole course of his studies in the faculty of law at Cairo University in the late 1940s and early 1950s, there was only one student who used a private car, and he was the son of Ismail Pasha Taymur, chief confidential secretary at the Royal Palace.

When I began teaching in the faculty of law at Ain Shams University in the mid-1960s, I was thirty years old, had a doctorate, was married and lived far from my place of work in al-'Abbasiya. Still, it never occurred to me, even at that time, to have my own car. It seemed natural that I should take the Helwan train as far as Bab al-'Luq, then the trolley bus to al-'Abbasiya. Almost all my colleagues in the faculty were doing the same thing, the only owners of private cars being the dean and the senior professors.

After I had been teaching at the university for four years, a friend who was emigrating to Scotland offered to sell me his car, a 1957 Austin, for four hundred pounds, which I would pay in installments over ten months. That sum was the most I could afford to spend on such a thing at that time. I did buy the car, but I do not remember that I derived much pleasure from it. It often needed a hefty push to get it started, my students in the law faculty regularly performing this service for me at the end of the day. To make matters worse the gatekeeper never paid me any attention when I passed through the university gate in my car, whereas he stood to attention for a colleague of mine who came to university driving a Mercedes acquired after working in the Gulf. My colleague's appearance was not at all compatible with the Mercedes. He was so small and it so big that he had to sit up high in order to see what was happening in front of the car. The gatekeeper's salute and respect were clearly meant for the car and not its owner, just as the lack of respect directed toward me was not aimed at my person but at my ancient Austin.

That was an early indication of what would transpire in Egypt. After a few years' absence from Egypt, I came back in the mid-1970s to find that many junior faculty members had acquired their own cars, and had come to regard a car as one of the necessities without which life would be intolerable. After a few more years, the two- or three-car family made its appearance, with sons and daughters insisting each on having his or her own car. If you go to Cairo University today you will see hundreds of private cars packed together in row after row, waiting for their twenty-year-old owners to come out of their lectures. How different from the time when my father used to arrive at the faculty of arts to deliver his lectures and assume his responsibilities as the dean of the faculty by bus or metro.

A vicious circle has been created: a deterioration in the efficiency and availability of public transport has led to an increase in the number of private cars, which in turn has led to the further neglect of public transport as well as to the ever slower pace of public buses along the clogged arteries of the city. With the increase in the number of private cars, public transport has become associated more and more with the lower classes, whose need for transportation can be more easily ignored by the government than those of classes with more influence. Thus while the government seems to spare no effort and withhold no expense to build new overpasses and provide facilities for private motorists, much less effort and expense is spent on improving public transport.

But there is, of course, an important and powerful reason for the growth in the number of private cars that we have not yet properly examined. Some time between the early 1960s and late 1970s the private car went from being simply a means of transport to being a status symbol. With the introduction in the mid-1970s of a more liberal system of importation, Egypt was suddenly transformed into a magnificent showroom for different types of cars from all over the world. This created new opportunities for vaunting and vain display, to say nothing of the various accessories with which modern cars are now equipped, and it became possible for anyone who had spent a few years in the Gulf to return with this precious symbol of success. Specific models of car now denote specific types of social advancement within different income groups. Not all cars have the same degree of glamor but they all, with their various degrees, affirm the principle of advancement itself. This was hardly possible in the 1960s and early 1970s when the choice was limited to two humble models of Egyptian-made car. Automobile advertisements now have to specify which of the various comforts and amenities exist in the cars on offer, and some cars are even designated by distinctive nicknames which identify the age and degree of expense of cars of the same make. Different models of Mercedes, for example, are nicknamed 'the sow,' 'the parson's nose,' and 'the phantom,' making it possible to rank their owners more precisely.

The inability to purchase a car has thus come to be regarded as a sign of failure. It is now quite common to come across members of the middle class, especially adolescents, who have never set foot on a bus or other means of public transport; and the sight of a young man, no more than eighteen years of age, driving a car the price of which might exceed one or two hundred thousand pounds has become a familiar one on the main streets of Cairo, or on the roads linking the captial to the tourist villages on the north coast or the Red Sea. For a fast growing segment of the Egyptian population there is probably no better symbol today of social advancement than the private car. For one thing, it is something that everyone can see. As a means of publicly displaying and vaunting wealth, it is superior to a house or to socializing in expensive restaurants because it is seen by people outside the immediate social circle. A car is also more conspicuous than jewelry, and the prices of different types of cars are well known, leaving little room for doubt about the owner's financial capacity.

We have reached the point today where the private car, even though it has effectively lost its function as an efficient means of locomotion within the city, has held on to its function as a symbol of social advancement. What is important here is not the amount of comfort the car may bring but the very fact of its purchase and possession. This is, of course, no different from all the other things that perform little more useful function in our lives than to excite envy or admiration among our acquaintances and neighbors.

10

Weddings

I don't recall attending a single wedding celebration during the 1940s and 1950s that was held in a hotel. Weddings were traditionally held in the homes of the families concerned. If the house was too small to accommodate all the invited guests, marquees that could accommodate any number of people would be erected in the garden or on the roof of the building. Nor do I recall seeing cameras at any of the weddings of my childhood. Either before or after the wedding ceremony, the bride and groom would go to a photography studio, and some photographs would be taken which would afterward be framed and hung on the wall for ever. Even music did not have an important role at middle-class weddings, let alone belly-dancing, about which I knew nothing at that time other than what I had learned from the cinema. While the figure of the seamstress coming and going was an important one—the custom of buying a wedding dress was not yet widespread—girls had not yet heard of the coiffeur, who today occupies such an important position in the preparations for every wedding, and whose charges constitute a not inconsiderable part of its costs.

The years passed and I began to receive invitations to attend the weddings of my students or the sons and daughters of my friends, nearly all of them held in one of Cairo's large hotels. In the 1940s and 1950s hotels did not play any role worth mentioning in our lives, for tourism was not significant, and there were fewer large hotels capable of hosting wedding parties. Even if more hotels had existed, it would have never occurred to anyone to marry their son or daughter anywhere other than at home. For what did the party require that could not be provided at home, and in any case, how was a real *farah* (the Arabic word for 'wedding' also means 'joy' and 'merriment') conceivable without neighbors around to witness the goings-on in the happy home, and the entire street resounding with the women's trilling cries of joy?

It was in the early 1970s that the wealthier classes began to hold wedding parties in the large hotels, and this gradually changed the nature of the wedding ceremony. Some rituals were eliminated and others introduced so that a legitimate fear arose of Egyptian wedding customs that had survived for centuries disappearing and being replaced by rites and rituals determined solely by the mangers of those large hotels. I have noticed for instance, that the celebratory ululations of women, the *zaghruta*, are scarcely heard, if at all, at these hotel parties. This may be because the sort of women who attend weddings in hotels are not proficient at unleashing these shrill cries, or they may regard the custom as beneath them. Or it may be because a hotel wedding is attended only by invited guests—there are no neighbors to inform of the happy occasion by means of the *zaghruta*.

A similar fate faced *milabbis,* (sugar-coated almonds), and has almost overtaken *sharbat* (a drink made of diluted, flavored syrup). To Egyptians, there is a strong association between the celebration of any happy event and the eating and drinking of exceedingly sweet food and drinks, perhaps because of the scarcity of sugar in the daily diet, including fruit. No wonder that Egyptians often refer to the rarity of a thing by calling it a 'fruit.' It is appropriate then that great lengths are gone to to sweeten the *sharbat* and pass around the *milabbis,* so that the 'sweetness' of the wedding and its delight might be felt all the more strongly. The splendor of the *milabbis* container was one of the principal means by which the upper classes distinguished themselves from the lower. In hotel weddings, however, if the *milabbis* features at all, it makes an embarrassed appearance as if the remnant of a custom on its way to extinction. As for the *sharbat*, Western taste, which regards its sweetness as excessive, has gradually imposed itself so that the drink is either forgotten or mixed with a good measure of fruit juice.

It must also be the hotel managers who insist that children should not attend these weddings. Many people would regard this as most regrettable, for how can a wedding be complete with no children around? But it seems that the managers of hotels fear that the reins may slip from their hands and that they may not be in complete control of the quantity of food consumed, or of the execution of the steps and rituals of the celebration in the planned order. Consequently, awful expressions are often added to wedding invitations such as: "It is requested that you not bring children along with you," or "We wish your children a pleasant sleep," this, of course, being the last thing that the children want to do on the day of a wedding.

What, however, is beyond any explanation is the hideous amplification of the music and singing that are invariably to be experienced at these hotel weddings. There you are in one of the grandest hotels in Cairo, sitting at a glorious celebration on which no money or effort has been spared to make it as beautiful and as perfect as can be, surrounded by some of the most important people in the country, including present and former prime ministers and the leading figures in politics and business, but unable to utter a single word to your neighbour because of the deafening music. On some occasions, where the person footing the bill has been a close relative or friend, I have suggested controlling this aspect of the celebrations, only to discover that the father of the bride or groom is, like myself, incapable of reducing the sound one iota. Matters proceed in accordance with a higher will

unknown to any of us. I have found no convincing explanations for this phenomenon. It has been suggested, for
instance, that Egyptians have a natural predilection for
boisterousness and are not disturbed by loud noise. This
is not a satisfactory explanation, for the pain is visible on
the faces of the people seated there. Surely one cannot
imagine any person, Egyptian or otherwise, deriving
pleasure from festivities in which one is forced to sit as
silent as a statue. It has also been suggested that the very
loud noise performs the useful function of disguising the
poor performance of the singers or musicians. But this
does not follow for the weddings on which tens of thousands of pounds have been spent and for which only the
best bands and the best singers have been recruited. What
seems certain is that both bride and groom as well as their
parents, not to mention the poor invited guests, have lost
all control over what is taking place. Whoever is in
charge of the volume of the music and all other arrange-
ments has apparently issued his instructions and is probably not even present at the celebration.

A similar powerlessness reigns where the video photographer is concerned. The bride and groom are prepared
to submit fully to his instructions. They and their two
families are quite aware of the importance of what he is
doing. For the judgment of future generations on this
wedding ceremony seems largely to depend on it. The
photographer alone knows the poses and angles in which
the bride and groom appear in the most splendid light, in
which the groom appears happy and delighted with his
bride, and the bride beautiful and delighted with her

groom. Only the video film will remain once all the ceremonies are over and everyone has departed. It is also the
only proof of the sum of money spent on the wedding. It
is the only proof that for instance, the dancer was really
Fifi Abdu or Dina, and not anybody else, that the singer
was Amr Diab and not another, for who can contest the
truth of the combination of both sight and sound? There
is thus no end to the trouble to which the bride and
groom may be put to for the sake of producing that film
in the most perfect manner. The initial ceremonial procession is drawn out until everyone is bored to death; the
bride and groom's steps must be slow enough for the film
to be used up, and for the guests it is like watching a the-
atrical performance in which the dramatic representation
of a scene is repeatedly acted before the camera until the
screen-director is completely satisfied with the level of
performance. The guests, for their part, must watch out
not to trip over the cables spread out all over the floor,
and be careful not to speak to the bride or groom for
longer than necessary when the camera is trained on
them. A friend swore to me recently that a family he
knows suffered tremendous shock and profound misery
when they discovered after their daughter's wedding that
the video film had been damaged, and that there was no
record of the ceremony. They felt compelled to reenact
the whole ceremony in order to have the film after all.
Hearing such stories, one would be forgiven for thinking
that the possession of a video film had become a condition of marriage without which it is not legally valid.

In short, in its transfer from the private home to the

hotel, the wedding ceremony has very nearly passed out of the control of the bride and groom's family. It is true that they are required to make some initial choices from among options presented to them. They may choose this or that dancer or singer, a European ceremonial procession or a native or a Nubian one, and then there are various menus to chose from. But once the person who is footing the bill makes their choice according to their ability to pay, the whole thing is entrusted to the hotel management including all sorts of 'technical' details which are too many and too complicated to be explained beforehand. From that point onward, the parents of the bride and groom are treated like any other guests; they sit where they are told to and leave their designated spot only when the dancer, singer or video photographer asks them to perform a certain task, such as kissing the bride or the groom.

What is it exactly that compels people to be so submissive and compliant, and why, in any case, was the practice of holding wedding parties in private homes abandoned? It may be thought that the reason lies in the scarcity of spacious homes with sufficiently large gardens to accommodate all the guests, now that living in apartments is the norm, even among the upper classes. But if this was the reason, why then do so many people who own splendid villas with spacious gardens, or rooftops large enough to accommodate hundreds of guests resort to staging these parties in hotels? A more likely explanation may be the proliferation of new goods and services that have come to be required for a wedding and that can only be easily provided for by a large hotel. Only such hotels can comfortably arrange for the attendance of so many musicians accompanying the singer or dancer, and for all the complicated electrical equipment for transmitting sound and producing video films. Hotels alone can stage that awesome scene in which the bride and groom are enveloped in smoke that is supposed to resemble a cloud. Only a hotel administration apparently has the necessary expertise regarding the correct height of the wedding cake, the appropriate types of flowers, as well as of food and drink, and so on. In fact a whole science of wedding protocol appears to have evolved that is far beyond the capacity of any ordinary father or mother. The managers of large hotels alone are party to such esoteric knowledge.

There is a sense in which when people decide to stage a wedding ceremony in a hotel, they are really not holding a party, but are rather 'purchasing' one. Someone has very wisely said that in our modern technological society, 'verbs', or actions, are increasingly becoming 'nouns,' or objects. Thus, the act of walking has been transformed into the motor car, the act of washing into the automatic washing machine, and conversing with the family into the television set. Similarly, with wedding parties you are no longer celebrating a marriage but buying one, you do not discuss designs with a seamstress but go out and purchase a wedding dress, and dancing and singing are performed for the sake of producing a video tape. You no longer utter the *zaghruta* or laugh or even talk, for modern electrical equipment has left little space for the pursuit of such activities.

One should not, however, belittle one important function performed by hotel weddings: complete protection and safety from the outside world. Over the last two decades, wealthy Egyptians have begun to surround their residences with high walls that cannot easily be scaled. They have also started to employ private firms to provide full time security guards to protect their properties. These guards spend the entire night outside these people's houses in wooden booths that in the past were only seen in front of the houses of cabinet ministers. In like fashion, it is now deemed necessary for the wedding parties of the new Egyptian middle class to be shielded from any mischievous or envious persons who might in any way disturb this festive event. Key suspects would be neighbors who may, until recently, have belonged to the same class as the people putting on the wedding, but are now considered to have declined greatly in relative social status.

One more important reason for holding weddings in hotels is the very high cost involved. There is of course a well-known economic law that the demand for a commodity decreases as its price increases. Economists have long recognized, however, that consumers may desire a high-priced commodity for no other reason than its high price, since this offers them the chance to display their ability to purchase it. If you are eager that people should be aware of how much wealth you have achieved, then what better way than to lavish money on a wedding ceremony in one of the large hotels, the rough cost of which is known to everyone? The wedding of a daughter or son is indeed the opportunity of a lifetime for apprising people of your success. It may even be one of the few such means available to the *nouveaux riches,* since neither education nor proficiency in a foreign language, nor even knowledge of the etiquette of social intercourse employed by the old upper class, is available to them. Even when attired in the most splendid clothes and adorned with the most expensive jewelry, a slight movement of the hand or a single word may betray them. How else can they convince people that they really belong to the upper class, except by staging magnificent celebrations for their children in grand hotels?

11

Summer Vacations

The concept of the summer vacation is of course known to most nations of the world, but it does have features and meanings peculiar to Egyptians, who have even coined a special word for it. These special features find their origins in Egyptian history and geography, as well as in Egypt's class structure, and have led the summer vacations to acquire a degree of importance for the Egyptian people which cannot perhaps be found elsewhere.

According to Gamal Hamdan, Egypt has "an extreme continental climate," characterized by a "sharply defined binary seasonality," while Egypt's topography renders her "wide open to the Mediterranean sea, without barriers or obstructions, and unalterably linked to it in both the human and physical aspects."[13] Socially speaking, summer holidaying in Egypt has been characterized, like many other aspects of social life, by a striking dualism reflecting an obvious contrast in the way of life of the upper and lower classes. No wonder that Egyptians have coined several words based on the noun for the summer season, *sayf*. Thus, where an English- or Frenchman would speak of "taking his holiday," the Egyptian speaks of *tasyif*, "summer holidaymaking," which means, specifically, spending the summer at the seaside. Egyptians even have a special noun for people who spend the summer in this way: *mustafin* or *musayifin*, as well as a word for the summer breeze, meaning, literally, the 'breeze that comes from the direction of the sea,' *bahari*, whose praises are continuously being sung. Egyptians attribute to it the power of restoring the soul and of healing the sick, they may even entrust it with carrying messages to and from a beloved person.

When I began to recall my old memories of summer vacations, I found that they shed an interesting light on some of the important changes that have taken place in Egypt's class structure. Prior to the July 1952 revolution, newspapers and magazines were often full of reports about which high society families had and which had not gone to Alexandria for the summer, and what Alexandria had done in preparation for its summer visitors. Nevertheless, all this fuss revolved around only a very tiny proportion of the Egyptian population, the same minority that Nasser used to refer to when he talked about the "half of one percent" of the population that dominated Egypt's wealth before the revolution. As for the rest of the population, the great majority were peasants who rarely left their villages, either in summer or during any other season. These villages were, by the communications standards of that time, very far away from the sea. Their inhabitants still sang the praises of the summer breeze, and went in search of it, finding the breeze that came from the direction of the sea available to them on the banks of the Nile and the many canals that branched out of it. As a matter of fact, when most Egyptians referred to the 'sea,' *bahr*, it was the Nile and its canals that they were talking about. As for the real sea, they called it 'the salty one,' and it was something that inspired great awe provoked, presumably by ignorance of it and a lack of any direct experience with it, and no realistic hope of ever seeing it.

For the small percentage of Egyptians whose news occupied a much greater proportion of the newspapers and magazines than was warranted by their real number, summer holidaymaking meant virtually one thing only: going to Alexandria. At that time there were virtually no other summer resorts in Egypt. There are two small exceptions to this. A tiny number of very rich families would spend the summer months in Europe. The other exception to Alexandria was Ras al-Barr, the temporary resort to which Egyptian high society retreated for their summer vacations during the Second World War, when Alexandria was threatened by the advance from the western desert of German and Italian troops. Ras al-Barr was a small resort situated between the Mediterranean and the furthest point to the north of the eastern branch of the Nile Delta. It was put up afresh every summer and then dismantled in the autumn. For a few summers, the charming huts and well-appointed hotels of Ras el-Barr, all built of wood and straw, received the richest and most important people in Egypt's social and political life.

Apart from these two exceptions, summer holidaying in Egypt meant going to Alexandria, and this city consequently enjoyed a degree of indulgence that no other Egyptian city can ever have known. Songs praised its beauty and the charm of its young women as they walked along the beach, while newspapers and magazines competed to invent new pet names for it. Sometimes Alexandria would be called 'the bride of the sea,' and at others simply the 'mouth,' meaning the mouth of Egypt. One adventurous Egyptian film maker in the late 1940s attempted to rebel against this monopoly on people's affections held by Alexandria, and produced a film set in another town on the Mediterranean, namely Marsa Matruh, an attractive city in its own right. The film was called *Shati' al-gharam* (The Beach of Passion), and featured the famous singer Layla Murad, one of whose songs extolling the beauty of Marsa Matruh's air and water became very popular. On seeing that film, Egyptians reacted as if they had never heard of Marsa Matruh before in their lives. The lead actor, Husayn Sidqi, played the role of a government employee working in Marsa Matruh, but to the Egyptian audience he had been severely punished to have been banished to such a distant town, three hundred kilometers away from Alexandria.

To the great majority of Alexandria's summer visitors only a very small section of the city, called _al-Raml_, or literally 'the sands' was at all familiar. This consisted of a few modern districts that contained many grand villas built largely by the rich foreign communities who had come to Egypt over the previous hundred years. The most famous of those districts had European names, such as Stanley and Glimonopolo, but they also included Sidi Bishr, a relatively new district built by the pre-revolution middle class. These districts grew rapidly in response to the needs of summer holidaymakers, but they were all situated outside the old working city of Alexandria where the daily activities of the city's inhabitants took place. One particular beach, hardly more than five hundred meters long, attained great fame and was given the apt name of Miami. It was undoubtedly the most attractive of the beaches of Alexandria, for it had, at an appropriate distance from the beach, a long island that ran parallel to the beach and protected the swimmers from big waves. In compliance with the needs of the upper class that frequented this beach, the government had built along it a row of attractive wooden huts, called 'cabins.' They were in fact more like luxurious little villas than beach cabins, containing all the requirements for luxurious living including wide balconies that allowed those sitting in them to watch, and be watched by, people from their own class strolling along the beach. The young women and girls of Miami Beach behaved just as they would have on the French Riviera, whether it was the swimming suits they wore or the kind of food and drink they consumed as they lounged on the sand. They were completely protected from any form of harassment or disturbance that could come from the lower classes, for the government had imposed an entrance fee of three piastres for getting onto the beach, an amount sufficient to exclude the great majority of the Egyptian population.

My father used sometimes to rent a flat not far from Miami Beach, for two or three months in the summer, and I must confess that it was always tempting for us boys to take advantage of finding the guard otherwise engaged, and sneak onto the beach without paying. In this way, we had the opportunity every now and then to view Egypt's high society at play, and even to share their pleasure of swimming in that gorgeous water. My father was not regarded as part of this class; most of its members were large landowners and he was only a university professor. But my mother had a rather different reason for not going to the beach; nothing would have persuaded her to appear among those half-naked people in her pitch-black dress and black headscarf. If my mother wished to go into the sea (and she believed firmly in the power of sea water to cure any ailment) she would get up at five o'clock in the morning, wake her maid, and go with her to the beach when there was not a soul to be seen. The maid's job was to come into the water with a robe or a very large towel with which my mother could cover herself, so that not an inch of her body, other than her face, would be seen. Some illustrated weekly magazines, such as *Akhir sa'a,*

124

al-Musawwar, or *al-Ithnayn,* often published caricatures of a well-known Azhari shaykh, al-Shaykh Abu al-'Uyun, who once dared to criticize women of the upper classes for allowing themselves to sit on the beach in their swimming suits. These publications ridiculed him for several years, taking him as the ultimate symbol of narrow-mindedness and fanaticism.

The season for summer holidaymaking was much longer then than it is today. One- or two-day visits to the coast were then hardly known, nor did Egyptians know, at that time, what a 'weekend' really was. Summer holidaymaking meant a long journey and a long absence. It involved taking a copious number of suitcases and trunks, and perhaps even matresses, blankets, and the like. The great majority of summer holidaymakers were either absentee owners of agricultural land, self-employed professionals who scheduled their workdays at their own convenience, or senior government officials who were not accountable to anyone. The government itself moved its headquarters and main offices to Alexandria at the beginning of every summer and returned to Cairo at its end. During these summer months it would attend to its more basic duties in the service of a limited number of people who were themselves close by in Alexandria. The king was also nearby in his magnificent Muntaza Palace, where he was supposed to be performing his official duties but actually spent most of the time gambling and receiving his women friends. Those working in the private sector but not running their own businesses, and therefore subject to other people's dictates with regard to the length of their holidays, were, as we have already seen, a very small proportion of the population until the 1970s.

Immediately after the 1952 revolution, the government removed many of the barriers that prevented many Egyptians from reaching the beaches of Alexandria. The abolition of the three-piastre fee, for example, was enough to allow for crowds of people to flood on to Miami and similar beaches, carrying with them everything that they might need for eating, drinking, playing, and sometimes even for cooking. Many of them held to their rules of modesty while swimming. Even Muntaza, which had been heavily guarded by armed soldiers who would stop anyone from going within twenty meters of the high walls of the palace, now had its gates wide open for the common people to enter and walk around its magnificent gardens. All were now allowed to come in to look for the gazelles that frolicked among the trees and to bring their bats and balls if they so wished. They were even permitted to go inside the palace itself to see the king's bed chamber and closets just as he left them when he was forced to abdicate.

It is not difficult for the reader to imagine the panic that struck the upper class in the first few months after the July revolution. Many members of this elite simply vanished from sight in fear of what the new government might bring in the way of further insults and humiliation. They also had to look for new places in which they could spend the summer months. Some of them found what they were looking for on the beaches of 'Agami, fifteen kilometers or so to the west of Alexandria, far enough to prevent most Egyptian holidaymakers from reaching it as that sort of distance required a private car. "Agamists' also had to have the inclination and the aptitude for mixing with the foreigners who had been the first to discover the 'Agami beaches, as manifested in the names given to those beaches: such as Blace, Bianci and Hannouville.

It was not long however, before the revolution produced its own upper class, for it was inevitable that the new elite of army officers and others who benefited from the revolution would want to distinguish itself from the rest of the people as well as to enjoy the fruits of their newly acquired power. The first of the beaches chosen by this new upper class was Ma'mura beach, situated immediately to the east of the Muntaza Palace. Ma'mura had no less in beauty and charm than Miami, it was even more spacious and green, and initially, its gates were left open to anyone who wanted to enjoy the beach, but before long the new elite felt it necessary to protect itself from intruders. An entrance fee was imposed on anyone who didn't own a flat or rent one of the attractive 'chalets' built by the government and made available to those close to the seats of power at nominal prices. The chalets, incidentally, were built in groups with names that had a more nationalist ring to them, like Salah al-Din and other heroes of Arab history, than the old names of Miami and Stanley.

Nor could the successive revolutionary governments resist the importunate demands by this new class for special privileges in the use of the beaches of Muntaza Palace itself, in spite of the fact that the opening to the general public of the grounds around the palace had originally been one of the most potent symbols of the egalitarian nature of the post-revolution government. New chalets and cabins went up along the Muntaza beaches, which were now given pharaonic names like Semiramis, Cleopatra and 'Aida—which, though only a name of an opera, was connected in people's minds with the glory of ancient Egypt. These new chalets and cabins were distributed among the especially privileged of the new elite, and the extensive beaches became heavily guarded once more, to prevent their being disturbed by the general public. So as not to appear that it was betraying its revolutionary principles, the government allowed the public to walk in the gardens for a relatively modest fee, and to swim off an extremely small part of the coast of Muntaza. The ludicrous contrast between this very narrow stretch of sand allowed to the masses, and the vast stretches of beach reserved for the small number of elite families was there for all to see, and differed little from the exclusiveness of the pre-revolution era.

Ma'mura beach continued to be the liveliest and fastest growing beach near Alexandria until the end of the 1960s, when it became clear that it had reached saturation point. But the number of people who could afford an Alexandria summer holiday went on growing, and accelerated in the inflation age of the 1970s. The growing numbers looked for new places in which to spend the summer, and could find no better place than 'Agami. They arrived in their droves to demand their right to the water and sea air, and disturb the scattered remnants of the old upper class, who were shut up in their peaceful villas along its beaches. At first the old upper class tried to muster their ranks and to create protected areas for their exclusive use. They created some imaginary club, whose membership would allow only the old inhabitants of 'Agami to use certain specified areas of beach, protected by hired guards. Within this area, they thought they could continue to wear their western-style swimming suits and to drink their alcohol. But this quickly proved to be highly unrealistic, since the eyes of the descending masses devoured them from all sides, gazing at them with disapproval, and wondering how such strange creatures could still exist. The impossibility of dividing the sea itself made it unrealistic for the old guard to try to protect themselves from prying eyes.

By the time those who made their wealth in the oil-rich nations of the Gulf, in the 1980s, came along to demand their right to a stretch of the north coast, the beaches of Ma'mura, Muntaza and 'Agami were all full. So this new generation of *nouveaux riches* went further west to build one new 'village,' as these settlements were called, after another. These compounds bore little resemblance to any real village, for they were neither green nor in any sense productive. They were hardly even inhabited, for most of this new breed of summer holidaymakers derived their incomes and wealth neither from agriculture nor from government jobs, but from their own private businesses outside agriculture. Such occupations did not allow them the long vacations that had been available to the old rich. They were continuously on the move, buying and selling, and could hardly afford to relax for long on the beach, but their cars allowed them to make short, quick visits to their new summer dwellings. In many cases, their main purpose in building or buying these dwellings in the first place had more to do with profitable investment than holidaymaking. Thus, summer holidaymaking was transformed at their hands, as with everything else they undertook, into another investment project.

It was only natural that during those four decades, from the early 1950s to the late 1980s, a new super-rich should emerge from out of all those sections of the population who climbed up the social ladder thanks either to new political developments or to economic change. These super-rich derived their wealth from a mixture of all the sources that I have mentioned: close connections with the centers of power, inflation and open-door policies, migration, and so-on. None of the beaches of Alexandria or to the west of it would do for this 'truly upper class,' even had there been room for them. A completely new beach had to be created, a new *sea* if that was at all possible, with dams and breakwaters to transform the heaving sea into calm lakes. Along this new beach, grand villas were constructed which combined the architectural styles of the villas of American movie stars in southern California, those of the rich Gulf Arabs, and those of the old Egyptian upper class. Behind them stood rows of smaller villas, built for those who had reaped slightly less benefit from pulling the strings of power, or exploiting the new economic environment. This was the idea behind the building of the village of 'Marina,' some one hundred kilometers west of Alexandria and about thirty kilometers east of Alamein. A towering perimeter wall was built around it with highly efficient guards standing at its gates to prevent the entry of anyone unable to prove their connection with one of the Marina owners or to pay the ten-pound entrance fee. In any case, since no one could reach the gates of Marina without a car—also necessary for moving around its vast area—the inhabitants of Marina were guaranteed the privacy and exclusivity they sought.

It is worth noting the points of similarity between the Marina of the 1990s and the Miami of the 1940s. Both have foreign names, high walls, and heavy guarding. In both cases the beneficiaries are a tiny proportion of Egyptian society, constituting a closed society of its own, its members intermarrying and doing business with each other. But there are also some important differences. For with the great technological progress that has occurred over the past fifty years, it is no longer enough for summer holidaymakers to lie on the sand for hours chatting or sipping beer. The boys and girls today need the excitement of their motorboats and jetskis on which to plough through the waves, exhibiting the magnitude of their parents' wealth.

12

The Cinema

Although I have often accompanied my children to the cinema, either at their insistence or at my own suggestion, the one and only time my father took me to the cinema was a momentous occasion.

My father was already over forty when the first Egyptian film was produced; what else, then, could one have expected of him? As for that great film which my father thought he had to see, it was nothing but a Walt Disney cartoon picture, by the name of *Pinocchio*. It seems that my father had heard about the film from one of his friends, who also told him that it was rather philosophical and that, although mainly addressed to children, it was important for somebody like him to see it. I still remember sitting beside my father in the second or third row, only four or five meters away from the screen so that he, with his very weak eyesight, could see the picture. I no longer remember the story of the film nor did I ever discover exactly what my father got out of it.

As for my own generation, there is no doubt that the cinema had a formative influence on us. I still remember the difficulty of trying to decide with my brother Husayn, who is two and a half years older than me, how best to approach my father so that he would be willing to give us the money for the cinema tickets. There was an open-air theater near our house in Heliopolis, which in the early 1940s was called the San Stefano Cinema. On the birth of King Faruq's first daughter, it was renamed the Ferial Cinema, and again Tahrir ('Liberation') Cinema after the 1952 revolution, before finally vanishing altogether.

The price of the cinema ticket at that time was only two and a half piasters (or five half-piaster pieces as we used to say) and this, by itself, should not have been an insurmountable obstacle in getting my father's permission to go to the cinema. The real obstacle was my father's deep conviction that it was all a waste of precious time, which would have been much better spent reading a book. But my father was by no means a hard-hearted man, so he did give us the required five piasters from time to time. When we had been to the cinema only recently, and it was really unlikely that he would give us the money, the only solution was to go when it was dark to the building opposite the cinema, wait until the Nubian doorman left his place in front of the building, steal into the building and hurry up the stairs to the roof from where we could see the whole film. Occasionally, the doorman would feel that there was something untoward going on up there and would come up to chase us off. This was rare though. What was more common was for us to enter the cinema and be treated with due respect having paid the legal price.

Being so eager and impatient to see the film, we usually reached the cinema long before the show was supposed to begin, and had no choice but to sit through one song after another played for our benefit. Every time a new song started we would hope that it would be the last, only to discover that another followed. But sooner or later the film would begin, and it is difficult to describe the pleasure that we derived from seeing those magnificent films, some of which we went to see again and again until we learnt much of the screenplay by heart. I remember one film in particular called *al-Madi al-maghul* (The Unknown Past), which deeply moved us. It was the story of a married man, played by Ahmad Salim, who had a car accident on his way to work and lost his memory. His wife, Layla Murad, sang many sad songs grieving over her husband, who could not get back to her, having forgotten his address. Such were our tender hearts that we thought the film was worth seeing four or five times.

Unlike my father, my mother seemed to welcome any opportunity to accompany us to the cinema. She was a great one for crying, particularly in films starring Amina

Rizq. My mother would go to the cinema dressed in black, covering her hair with her black veil, almost exactly like what Amina Rizq wore in most of her films. After each film, my mother would recall the film's exhortations and pieces of wisdom, often concluding "By God, this film tells no other story but my own!" We would then laugh and express our surprise that a film containing such improbable events could possibly have any resemblance to our mother's life. But she would never be dissuaded.

Two or three years after the end of the Second World War, important things seemed to be happening to Egypt, bringing about symptoms of what came to be regarded as 'the American way of life.' It was at about that time my brother-in-law returned from a few years in the United States, and brought with him, as a present for me, a multicolored tie, which I could not imagine ever wearing. These were also the years that witnessed the appearance in Egypt of that wondrous American chewing gum Chiclets, and of nylon shirts which enjoyed such popularity that anything new or captivating (even a new tramway) came to be described as 'made of nylon.' Two wonderful coffee shops were also opened with the name 'À l'Américaine' and were situated at two of the busiest corners in the commercial center of Cairo, with hardly more than a hundred meters between them. One of their principal attractions was a small machine on the counter, with a handle which, when turned, spread whipped cream over a scrumptious plate of ice cream. My friends and I used to fix our meeting place in front of one of these two coffee shops, from where we would go to the Metro Cinema nearby; it had recently opened and was distinguished for the splendor of its décor, its unusual cleanliness, its employees dressed in red suits and hats, and for being the first air-conditioned cinema in Egypt.

The reader may easily imagine how we boys of thirteen and fourteen felt to be seeing films like *Bathing Beauties* with Esther Williams and other beautiful, healthy, and apparently happy girls, all in swimming suits, shown in color in a wonderfully cool theater. This first experience of 'the American way of life,' coincided with the arrival of a strange new drink offered in a bottle whose shape was unlike that of any bottle we had ever seen. This new drink had a captivating taste as well as an attractive name, and Coca-Cola quickly became another symbol of the good life. All Egyptians, but particularly those who belonged, like us, to the more privileged segment of the society, were suddenly exposed to a cultural onslaught that seemed to be coming from a number of directions, but all of which originated in the United States: fast food and Coca-Cola bottles in restaurants and coffee shops, big American cars in the streets, novel ways of presenting the news in the media, new types of songs on the radio, and Hollywood films in the cinema.

During the 1940s, the two most opulent and glamorous streets in the center of Cairo were Fu'ad I, and 'Imad al-Din streets, but during the following two decades they began to age and suffered an obvious decline in status. The old cinemas of 'Imad al-Din Street, such as Studio Misr and the Cosmo Cinema, were also supplanted by larger and more glamorous establishments like the Rivoli and Radio cinemas. These new, modern cinemas rarely showed an Egyptian film during the whole of the 1950s and 1960s, having been built with the specific goal of screening only the foreign films that now appealed to the newly acquired tastes of the rising classes exposed to the new wave of Westernization, or, more precisely, Americanization.

Many Egyptian films had now to address themselves to those new tastes, but some had also to cater for the demands of Egyptians who had not yet acquired the taste for foreign films or fully adjusted themselves to them. A new direction taken by Egyptian films during the 1950s and 1960s was to transform well-known novels written by prominent Egyptian writers, such as the novels of Ihsan Abd al-Quddus, Naguib Mahfouz, Yusuf Idris, Yusuf al-Siba'i, or Abd al-Rahman al-Sharqawi, into films. It is interesting to note how these films bear witness to the change that had occurred in Egypt's social structure: while the most popular pre-1950s actors such as Yusuf Wahbi, and the two Shakib sisters Zuzu and Mimi, belonged to upper-class families that had disowned them when they had taken to acting, most of the leading actors of the 1950s and 1960s, such as Shukri Sarhan, Farid Shawqi, Shadia, and Abd al-Halim Hafiz came from more humble social backgrounds. Throughout those two decades of the 1950s and 1960s, Egyptian films continued to be preoccupied with social problems but they were no longer obsessed with the problem of social dualism that dominated Egyptian films before the 1952 revolution. It suddenly appeared that there were things in life other than the stark contrast in Egyptian society between the extremes of wealth and poverty. There were also other important issues to tackle, such as the status of women, bureaucracy, and dictatorship as well as sexuality, of course. With the greater opening up to the West in the 1970s and 1980s, Egyptian films naturally followed in the footsteps of European and American cinema, allowing for more sexual permissiveness and violence as well as giving longer rein to their obsession with pure technique. We came therefore to see, and were obliged to admire, a new type of Egyptian film, where narrative content was lost for an obsession with technique and large doses of sex. Some films of this new style were produced by the same directors who had produced the films with socialist and nationalist leanings only ten years before.

When I sit today in front of the television to watch an old Egyptian film produced in the 1940s, with a beginning, an end, and a straightforward story in the middle, I sometimes catch myself on the verge of tears in sympathy with one or another of the characters in the film, exactly as my mother would when she saw the films of Amina Rizq. I find myself quite willing to forgive some excessive sentimentality if the film has what I consider to be the right message. I try to win my children over to my point of view and to have them share with me the pleasure of seeing these old films, but my efforts are usually in vain. They may pretend for a few minutes to be enjoying the film, but it is abundantly clear to me that they are watching it only for my sake, exactly as I used to do with my mother fifty years ago.

In an Egyptian film which was produced to wide acclaim in the early 1990s, the phenomenon of social dualism was again tackled but in a very different way from how it had been addressed fifty years earlier. In this film, *al-Mansi*, (The Forgotten One), the 'two nations' that constitute Egyptian society, are portrayed as two separate worlds, although they are physically divided by no more than a railway line. The title role is played by the most popular comedian of the 1990s, 'Adil Imam. He is a signalman on night shift in a signal box, who accidentally comes into contact with the beautiful office manager (Yusra) of a multimillionaire businessman (Karam Mutawi'). The day of their encounter is the birthday of the millionaire, who has invited wealthy Egyptian and foreign businessmen to a party in which he tries to fix his beautiful office manager up with an immensely wealthy man from a Gulf Arab state. This is done with the hope of facilitating a deal in which the Egyptian millionaire expects to make a few hundred million dollars. It is only coincidence that brings the 'modern' world of Yusra and the 'backward' world of 'Adil Imam together, the contrast between them allowing for all sorts of fascinating observations to emerge about the two 'nations,' the nature of their relationship, and how each world regards the other. The film ends with 'Adil Imam and Yusra's characters each returning, inevitably, to their own worlds, for there is really no basis upon which they can have any amiable relationship.

The phenomenon of social dualism has inspired Egyptian writers of novels, short stories, plays, and film scripts on and off over the last century. A very eloquent commentator on it was the actor, writer, and director Naguib al-Rihani, one of the most prominent figures in the history of Egyptian cinema and theater during the 1930s and 1940s. For al-Rihani, the problem was similar to that presented in *al-Mansi;* the division of Egyptian society into two classes: a small, thoroughly westernized class, and everyone else, with their more traditional ways of life. Like 'Adil Imam, al-Rihani found there was no real dialogue between the two, each preferring to avoid the other. But nothing, of course, remains exactly the same, and it is interesting to trace the change in this relationship as reflected in 'Adil Imam's contemporary depictions of social dualism compared with Naguib al-Rihani's, observed over fifty years earlier.

The first thing to note is the change in characteristics of the upper class as portrayed by al-Rihani and Imam. Members of the upper class in al-Rihani's films and plays were usually portrayed by fair skinned, round-faced actors with some reddish complexion pointing to the Turkish element in their blood. The upper classes in 'Adil Imam's films are mostly dark-skinned with indigenous Egyptian features who, were it not for the expensive materials from which their clothes are made, the types of cars they own, and the foreign words they deliberately drop into their speech, would easily pass as members of the general public.

There are also important differences in the sources of wealth of the two classes. While in al-Rihani's films and plays the upper classes were, almost without exception, big landowners, in 'Adil Imam's, the sources of income and wealth of the upper class are more dubious, ranging from brokerage activities to pimping. With Naguib al-Rihani, a member of the upper class was indeed often a parasitic unproductive person but the main source of his income and wealth, namely agriculture, was itself productive. But with 'Adil Imam, not only is the upper class parasitic but it derives its income and wealth from sources that are often morally tarnished. This important change in the nature of the sources of income and wealth has inevitably affected the portrayal of class relationships. In *al-Mansi*, the big businessman looks upon the downtrodden signalman with real hatred and fear, for in his eyes, this wretched creature represents his own recent past, which he is desperately trying to banish from his memory. In contrast, the upper class in al-Rihani's films often looked upon the poor either with genuine sympathy or with complete indifference.

One problem, for example, faced by one al-Rihani hero is that the pasha he works for can never remember his name. As much as the hero repeats that his name is Hamam (meaning pigeon), the pasha continues to forget it, using the name of every other bird instead. But the pasha does not have any feelings of fear or antipathy toward the poor fellow, for he feels secure, sees no threat to his social status and regards this social differentiation as part of the natural order of things. Such confidence has long ago disappeared. As we have seen, members of today's upper class feel compelled to surround them-selves with heavily armed guards to prevent any attempt by the likes of 'Adil Imam's signalman to approach their strongholds.

For all their close contact with Western culture, the older upper class, as represented in al-Rihani's films, had a strong sense of belonging to a cultural tradition of their own. This sense of belonging is largely absent with the upper classes of 'Adil Imam's films. The older upper class evaluated their income and wealth in Egyptian pounds, while today's upper class thinks mainly in dollars. Egypt was regarded by the older upper class as their only source of livelihood, but in the eyes of today's upper class the source of their wealth is largely foreign. Egyptian landowners of the 1930s and 1940s knew quite well, and were often even ready to admit, that the Egyptian peas-ant was the real source of their prosperity. In the eyes of today's ruling elite, however, the Egyptian peasant, along with the industrial laborer and the government employee, are something of a burden and a nuisance. Such people only eat and drink and reproduce, while burdening the state budget with their incessant demands for food subsi-dies which inevitably reduce what is available to spend on improving the country's infrastructure. The children of these lowly beings encroach on the beautiful beaches bringing such noise and ugliness with them that the beaches become almost uninhabitable. In short, as far as the newly portrayed upper class is concerned, the great majority of the Egyptian population have no real justification for living at all, and the world would be a much better place without them.

But there is apparently a limit beyond which social dualism cannot go without threatening social peace. In the early films and plays of Naguib al-Rihani, the story always ended with reconciliation between the two classes and with each party admitting its mistakes to the other. Thus the rich pasha would admit that it was the poor al-Rihani who was actually in the right, and the poor man would willingly accept whatever was offered to him and no more, so that peace would once again prevail. This was not the case however, in al-Rihani's very last film, *Ghazl al-Banat* (Cotton Candy), produced in 1949, for reconciliation no longer seemed possible. The poor tutor of the pasha's daughter realizes at the end of the film how naive he has been to imagine that the pasha's daughter could have been in love with him, so he sheds a few tears and goes on his way. By the late 1940s any other ending would have appeared rather contrived and far fetched, for by then social divisions had reached a point where some kind of explosion was inevitable. Indeed, the 1952 revolution came to put an end to al-Rihani's version of social dualism. But with Sadat's open-door policies, introduced in the early 1970s, social dualism started again to reassert itself. At first it seemed possible that peace could be maintained between the two poles of the social system. By the end of the 1980s however, this was clearly no longer possible and the relationship between the worlds

of 'Adil Imam and Karam Mutawi' could not end in reconciliation. *Al-Mansi* ends with the two parties lying in
wait for each other, with a strong suggestion of imminent
and violent confrontation.

13

Egyptian Economists

Before the First World War it was difficult to find Egyptians who specialized in economics. Yes, there were some writings on economic issues and was some teaching of economics in Egypt before then, but those who wrote and taught at that time did not regard themselves, nor were they regarded by others, as economists. The 1920s is therefore a reasonable starting point to take for tracing the development of the economic profession in Egypt.

The first generation of Egyptian economists (1920–45) consisted mostly of graduates of either the School of Law established by Isma'il Pasha in 1867, or the Teachers'

Training Institute, or the Higher School of Commerce. They were then sent to study abroad on state scholarships or privately financed, mainly in France and England, and returned to Egypt with doctorates in political economy to teach in the National University established in 1908, or to work in one of the banks or in the Ministry of Finance. They were generally well educated, had access to able teachers, and had read the key texts on economic theory in their original languages. The economic literature that this generation produced must now seem quite remarkable, considering the almost complete vacuum from which they emerged as far as economic literature in Arabic was concerned. They wrote mainly on Egypt's economic history, or on current economic problems, but in economic theory they did not advance beyond the writing of textbooks. The most prominent among them were Abd al-Hakim al-Rifa'i, Ahmad Nazmi Abd al-Hamid, Rashid al-Barrawy, Fahmi Lehayta, Abd al-Mon'im al-Kaysuni, and Wahib Messiha.

Nevertheless, economics in Egypt was handicapped at that time by major obstacles on both the supply and the demand sides. By obstacles on the supply side I mean that there was a shortage of human resources as well as of economic data. The number of Egyptians that could be called 'economists' at the beginning of this period could not have exceeded a dozen, and by the end of the period, at the end of the Second World War, could not have exceeded forty or fifty, and the majority of these were engaged in practical rather than academic work. Training in economics continued until the end of this period only as part of the wider study of law or business administration, and one could not become an economist without pursuing more specialized economic studies abroad. But state scholarships were limited and, in any case, the study of economics was not given priority, either by the state or by the Egyptian students themselves. But even had there been a good number of Egyptian economists, they would not have found much economic data with which to work. National accounts were not yet systematically collected even in industrialized countries until after the publication of Keynes' *General Theory* in 1936 and the increased demand for such data created by the Second World War. In Egypt too, it was the requirements of the war, and the Middle East Supply Center created to cope with them, that motivated the first serious efforts to collect and analyze national accounts. The most prominent of these efforts was undertaken during the last two years of this period (1944–45) and resulted in Mahmoud Anis's pioneering study, published in 1950 with the title "A Study of the National Income of Egypt."[14] This was one of the first steps on the long road of collecting and analyzing macroeconomic data in Egypt. Before it, there was very little data available on national income and expenditure, on consumption and investment, or, of course, on the pattern of income distribution. The size of gross domestic product, per capita income, or of their changes over time, were anybody's guess.

Egypt's efforts to collect reliable statistics though, were not inconsiderable compared with what other third world countries were achieving at the time. The

Department of Statistics and Census was established as a part of the Ministry of Finance as early as 1905, and started to publish *l'Annuaire Statistique* in 1909. The first population census had already been conducted in 1882, and fairly regular and accurate statistics on land owner-ship and what crops were being farmed were available in the early 1900s. This material was particularly rigorously compiled when it had anything to do with the cotton crop. In addition, regular accounts of government finances had been prepared since the beginning of the British occupation in 1882, with the main purpose of handling the external debt. None of this was sufficient, however, for any systematic study of the wider questions of economic development. This had to await the collec-tion and analysis of national accounts.

In addition to the shortage of human resources and of statistical data, there was a shortage of demand for the services of economists. Major economic decisions contin-ued to be taken throughout this period by the colonial power, whose aim was not so much the economic devel-opment of Egypt as efficient colonial administration. The latter function could be best performed by British experts in London, or British administrators and engineers work-ing in Egypt, with very little need for Egyptian econo-mists. The basic reforms of the tax system had already been carried out in the early days of the British occupa-tion and the task of economic development was limited virtually to raising the efficiency of Egyptian agriculture and particularly the production, financing, and marketing of cotton. This, of course, fell short of the aspirations of the Egyptians themselves, who wanted to see rising standards of living and a much more diversified economy, as well as additional tax reforms with wider coverage, greater progressiveness in tax rates, and more equity in the treatment of different types of income. It was taken for granted, however, that such reforms had to await political independence; until the British were out of the country, basic economic reforms could not be dealt with. What was needed then, or so it seemed, was not economists but lawyers and politicians able to argue Egypt's case in international conferences and around negotiation tables. The most popular and prestigious college during this period continued, therefore, to be the faculty of law and only very few felt a strong need for specialized training in economics.

Looking back at this interwar period, it seems natural that the meager economic literature produced by Egyptians at that time would be dominated by two subjects: agriculture (particularly cotton) and economic history. The former is explained by the overwhelming share of agriculture in Egypt's total economic output, labor force, and exports, and the latter, perhaps, by psychological factors. The frustration caused by foreign domination may have created an urge to relive the past, both as a source of consolation and as a possible guide to the future. Several excellent studies of Egypt's economic history were written during this period, and hardly surpassed in subsequent periods. It is interesting to note a similar phenomenon in other disciplines, for the same period also engendered excellent studies of Egyptian, Arab, and

Muslim political and intellectual history; the works of Ahmed Amin, Taha Husayn, al-Aqqad, and Muhammad Husayn Haykal on Islamic intellectual and political history, as well as the multi-volume work of Abd al-Rahman al-Rafi'i on Egypt's modern political history, are among the best known literature of this period.

The one important exception to the predominance of agriculture and economic history in the economic writing of that period was the work of Tal'at Harb. Here was a man who was looking to the future rather than the past, and obsessed with the development of industry rather than agriculture. Although he was much more a man of action than a scholar, his economic speeches, articles, and memoranda constitute an important landmark in the development of Egypt's economic literature, and are strongly reminiscent of Mercantilist literature in Europe and of the writings and practical achievements of Friedrich List in Germany in the first half of nineteenth century. Both Tal'at Harb and List saw no economic future for their respective countries without rapid industrialization and an active role for the government in protecting infant industries.[15]

Notwithstanding Tal'at Harb and other Egyptian economists' expression of the need for economic independence, most Egyptian economic writings of this period reflected a high degree of dependence on foreign scholarship. With virtually no predecessors in economic writing to fall back on (the only exception perhaps being that of Islamic jurists' writings on public finance) these Egyptian pioneers had to rely heavily on European and, to a lesser extent, American textbooks, as well as on studies of Egypt's own economic problems and history written by Europeans. The best books on Egypt's system of irrigation and agriculture that appeared during that period, were written by British engineers, while the best economic history of nineteenth-century Egypt, at least until the 1960s, was probably that of Crouchley.[16]

For all their shortcomings, this generation of Egyptian economists performed at least one great and lasting service for the discipline of economics in Egypt, namely their Arabizing of economic terms and concepts. Most of the terms we use today, whether in micro- or macro- economic theory, international trade, money and banking, insurance, or the history of economic thought, were coined during this inter-war period. Thanks to their excellent command of the rules of the Arabic language and their intimate acquaintance with the best examples of classical Arabic literature, the new terms this generation coined for the expression of economic concepts were linguistically correct, culturally appropriate, and clear and simple, thus easily absorbed and widely accepted.

The second generation of Egyptian economists (1945–70) was in many ways luckier than the first. Not only were the twenty-five years after the Second World War among the best years in economic terms for twentieth-century Egypt, but great leaps forward were also made in several areas connected with the economic profession.

Firstly, there was a rapid growth in the number of students receiving training in economics. Graduates of the two faculties of law and commerce from the old national university (Fu'ad I and later Cairo University), now ran into the hundreds every year, to whom were added, in the early postwar years, the graduates of Alexandria University established in 1942, followed by 'Ain Shams University in 1950, Assiut University in 1957, and the modernization of al-Azhar University to allow training in more subjects, including economics, in the 1960s. In 1960, the first faculty to specialize in economics and political science was opened in Cairo University.

Secondly, shortly after the 1952 revolution there was a great expansion in state scholarships for university graduates to pursue their studies abroad. The government's commitment to rapid economic development, industrialization, and central planning, and its pursuing of a policy of non-alignment between the mid-1950s and mid-1960s, resulted in its sending large numbers of graduates, including economics graduates, on state scholarships both to the East and the West, in the belief that a healthy balance could be achieved between the two rival ideologies. Many of these students were sent abroad for relatively long periods, up to five years or more, and the subject they studied was often determined by the government in accordance with the perceived needs of the country, a policy reminiscent of that of Muhammad Ali's scholarships more than a century earlier.

Thirdly, an equally ambitious and rigorous policy was pursued in the collection of statistics. A greatly expanded and modernized administration for the collection and analysis of statistical data, the Central Agency for Public

Mobilization and Statistics (CAPMAS), was for many years entrusted to energetic and well-educated army officers who performed a remarkable service to economic research.

The two major handicaps of the earlier period were thus largely overcome: well-trained economists were no longer in short supply, nor was there anything like the same degree of paucity of data, and both were now in demand. In addition to the old ministries of Finance and Commerce and the expanding universities, there was now a separate Ministry for the Economy, a new Ministry for Industry and a new Commission for National Planning which was later to become a Ministry of Planning. In the early 1960s, the National Planning Institute was conceived and directed by an energetic and brilliant astronomer, Ibrahim Hilmi Abd al-Rahman, who happened to be also interested in economic planning and to share the economic ambitions of the leaders of the 1952 revolution.

Looking back at the results of all this, even the most adamant believer in the principle of non-intervention must be impressed by what an expanded government role achieved in the field of economic information and research. A great wealth of new economic and social statistical data on Egypt became available, thanks largely to CAPMAS. Lectures, memoranda, and research papers on development problems and planning techniques were prepared and circulated by the Planning Commission and the Planning Institute. Translation was actively encouraged and subsidized by the state. Several non-Egyptian economists of high international standing were invited to Egypt to study, lecture, and write on the problems of the Egyptian economy, or the wider theoretical problems of economic development. Gottfried Haberler and Ragnar Nurkse were invited by the National Bank of Egypt in the early days after the 1952 revolution, to give public lectures on the problems of economic development in connection with international trade and capital formation. These later became the basis of some of their best known works. While the most radical measures of Nasser's socialism were being implemented, non-socialist economists of high international caliber were invited to Egypt for periods of varying length. Thus, it was in the early 1960s that Bent Hansen was sitting in his office in the National Planning Institute meeting Egyptian economists, conducting seminars, and writing his famous book on the Egyptian economy jointly with Girgis Marzouk.[17] During the same period, Patrick O'Brien, now a leading Oxford economic historian, was in Egypt writing a book on the transformation of Egypt's economic policy in the late 1950s and early 1960s. The book is still perhaps the best treatment of its subject.[18] The transformation to socialism also inspired an important study, in Arabic, of Egypt's economic history by Husayn Khallaf.

As well as the increase in quantity and the improvement in quality of applied work on the Egyptian economy during the 1950s and 1960s, these two decades can be regarded as the golden period for economic textbooks written in Arabic. The works of Sa'id al-Naggar on microeconomic theory, of Zaki Shafe'i on money and banking, of Zakariya Nasr on macro-economic theory and general economic history, of Labib Shukayr on international trade and Arab economic integration, and of Husayn Khallaf on public finance were all published during this time. They were lucid expositions of the established principles of economic theory and public finance, patiently and carefully written in correct and often stylish Arabic. The previous generation of Egyptian economists had made the bricks; this generation now used the bricks to build impressive structures.

This generation of economists enjoyed much greater stability than their successors would. Their periods abroad were long enough for them to take real advantage of their exposure to other cultures, and when they returned to Egypt with PhDs, they were given decent salaries and enjoyed the considerable prestige accorded to university professors in those days. They were neither hurried to publish nor were they subjected to the temptations of making great fortunes in an instant, the latter becoming possible only from the 1970s onward. This generation was not made of better metal than the next one, it was just not hit so hard.

The privileges enjoyed by these economists were also enjoyed by their contemporaries in literature and the arts. During the fifteen years or so following the Second World War, Egypt experienced a flowering of intellectual and artistic life comparable to that seen in the years after the First World War. This was when the best of Naguib Mahfouz and Yusuf Idris's work was published, and what many critics would regard as some of the best Egyptian plays, music, and fine arts produced during the whole century.[19] The combination of a strong and optimistic national movement, a reasonable degree of free expression, fairly good education, and a healthy interaction with foreign cultures, must have contributed to this.

As early as 1954, however, during the struggle for power between Nasser and Naguib, there were signs that this age of intellectual and artistic freedom would not last for long under a government that was not afraid to use a heavy hand to make people tow the line. By the mid-1960s, the combination of increased economic difficulties, foreign pressure, and the disastrous 1967 war led to state intervention on a new and ultimately unbearable scale.

This was reflected in the economics profession as much as anywhere else. From the mid-1950s onward, economists were increasingly expected to espouse the official ideology, not only in public life, but even in the intellectual environment of the universities. The government was not very clear at the beginning about what it wanted to do or even what it believed in, so rapidly changing and sometimes contradictory directives were given. Some academic economists allowed themselves to be dragged into this maze, following humbly in whatever direction the government chose to lead them. So it was that the cooperative system and Owen and Fourier became very popular subjects in the mid-1950s, planning in the late 1950s and Arab Socialism from 1961 onward, with touches of Marxism after 1964.

The government's insistence that its ideology be dominant in university instruction had a corrupting influence on economic scholarship in a number of ways. The weaker spirits in academia hurried to write whatever the government wanted to read, believing this to be the shortest route to public office. The more independently minded became discouraged, and some even preferred to leave Egypt altogether and look for jobs abroad rather than compromise their intellectual honesty. Even those who genuinely shared the government's commitment to socialism and comprehensive planning were soon to discover that public speeches and political intrigues were more rewarding politically and financially than scholarly work, and many were sorely tempted to leave their research work and go into politics.

The sad irony is that in the late 1950s, the government went so far as to insist that only its own brand of socialist ideology be discussed. In my opinion this had less to do with mere narrow mindedness than with the government's assessment of the requirements of international politics, but the result was disastrous all the same. Fearing that Egyptian Marxists could become mouthpieces of the Soviet Union, and perhaps even to show the U.S. that it could resist Soviet pressure, the Egyptian government put all Marxists of any influence in prison from 1959 to 1964. These included some of the most talented and best-trained Egyptian economists, such as Isma'il Sabri Abdallah, Fu'ad Mursi, and Fawzi Mansur, all of whom were university professors when they were arrested in 1959. After their release, those who were not denied the chance to return to academic life at all, found the new academic environment so discouraging that they gave up soon after returning to it. One important service to Marxist thought was, however, performed by Nasser, albeit inadvertently. For when Nasser started to arrest communists in 1959, one brilliant Egyptian economist made a narrow escape, ran away to France and later to West Africa, where he made important contributions to Marxist economic literature. Samir Amin is a prolific writer in French and his writings were almost immediately translated into English. Ironically, his work became accessible to Arab readers only through poor translations sold and circulated secretly in Egypt until well into the 1970s. When Samir Amin wrote a critique of Nasser's economic policy it had to be published in France under a pseudonym.[20] Since he could not return to Egypt until after the death of both Nasser and Sadat, his influence on economic thought and writing in Egypt has inevitably been small.

The factor which, directly or indirectly, had the most influence on how the economic thought of the next generation (1970–95) developed, was the military defeat of 1967. This was the generation of the October War, open-door policies, large oil revenues, inflation, the accumulation of a large external debt, peace treaties, structural adjustment, and most recently, the advocation of what is called a 'Middle East Market.' Many of these developments might have never taken place had the 1967 war not occurred. The Egyptian state was so weakened by the defeat that it lost much of its power to undertake new functions and felt obliged to loosen its grip on people's minds and freedom of expression. With widespread loss of faith in the state and its ability to fulfill its promises, its proclaimed ideology was bound to suffer. More important things than socialism, planning, and income distribution seemed now to be at stake.

For a while, Egyptian economists were preoccupied with calculating the economic losses resulting from the war, or with the problems of mobilizing resources for the war of attrition. However, attention soon moved to the new economic policy launched by President Sadat immediately after the October War of 1973. Over the following two decades, much of the energy of Egyptian economists was spent on either defending or criticizing the open-door policies. With the launching of the structural adjustment program in the mid-1980s, the controversy continued but with the emphasis now on such subjects as privatization and the elimination of government subsidies. These controversies led to the much greater involvement of Egyptian economists in public debate. Nothing like this could have arisen in the previous two periods. In the inter-war period, public debates on economic issues were made rare both by the scarcity of economists and by the relative stability of economic policies. In the 'socialist' period, economic policy was not debated but dictated. Now, even though public debates continued to have little influence on government decisions, the increase in the freedom of expression after 1970 and the sudden reorientation of economic policy after 1973 gave rise to debates between supporters and detractors of economic liberalization.

One of the things that transpired from this debate was the launching, by the Egyptian Economic Society in 1975, of an annual conference of Egyptian economists. The conference has been held regularly since then, and its published proceedings contain up-to-date analysis of the most topical of Egypt's economic problems. Here again we note a difference between this period and the previous two; for the first time since the birth of the discipline in Egypt, Egyptian economists are now the main source of analysis for the economic issues of their own country. During the inter-war period, most analysis of Egypt's economic problems came from British authors. Even in Nasser's years, the main works on the Egyptian economy continued to be written by foreigners. Now this is no longer the case. Important works exist, written by Egyptian economists in Arabic as well as in other languages, and references to Egyptian economists are increasingly made in the works of non-Egyptian scholars, while works of joint authorship between Egyptian and non-Egyptian economists is also quite common. Egyptian economists are also frequently called upon to contribute to international conferences and UN publications, and an increasing number of them occupy important positions in UN agencies. While important works by non-Egyptian authors continue to appear, it is no longer a one-way relationship in which Egyptian economists act as passive receivers of economic knowledge from abroad, even about their own country.

But for all the impetus that it gave to this generation of economists, the defeat of 1967 began by destroying the enthusiasm and confidence that had been responsible for much of the economic literature of the late 1950s, and early 1960s. With the withdrawal of state intervention in the economy, economists in many government departments found their services surplus to requirements and their prestige reduced. In the Ministry of Planning and the Planning Institute, for example, scores of well-trained economists found themselves suddenly redundant as a result of the decline in importance of the whole planning exercise. Five-year plans had long been abandoned for planning for one year at a time, and even when five-year plans were later restored, planning itself had become a much less serious exercise than it had been in the 1960s. University teachers faced frustrations of another kind in the apathy of students, partly from the military defeat and partly from the lower prospects of their obtaining good jobs after graduation. In addition, the government had to return to the policy of admitting large numbers into university, regardless of merit, as a way of appeasing a discontented populace. When the age of inflation arrived, following the increase in oil prices in 1973 and 1974, university teachers, like everybody else, were forced to look for ways of augmenting their income at the expense of their normal university duties. Although some good academic output continued to appear, and in greater volume than before, the general picture was one of a decline in the standard of scholarship.

All this is sometimes said to be part of the wider phenomenon of a general decline in moral standards associated with inflation and open-door policies, the sudden rise in new opportunities for making large fortunes, and the increase in the rate of social mobility. While all this may be true, another part of the explanation is the 'softening' of the state, the corruptive influence of which is at least as great as that of the previous despotism. All these developments in national universities are taking place under the government's nose and with its full knowledge, but no one seems to have sufficient power or motivation to put an end to it. Every year, the state awards what used to be the most prestigious prizes to economists who may have contributed very little to economic knowledge but happen to occupy, at the time of receiving the prize, ministerial or other political positions. By giving the prizes to non-deserving economists, the state is effectively withdrawing the honour from the deserving ones.

With the open-door policies, the state grew progressively softer, not only in domestic policies but also vis-à-vis foreign influence, and this had an important impact on the economy as a whole as well as on the economics profession. State scholarships virtually ceased, or were greatly reduced after 1967, and the financing of study abroad was gradually taken over by foreign governments, foundations, or companies. Remunerative research jobs were also made available by foreign institutions and consultancy offices within Egypt. The duration of study abroad became much shorter, giving the Egyptian student a particular technical skill but not necessarily the wider and deeper contact with foreign cultures that they would have had from the programs of the 1950s and 1960s. Also important is the fact that Egyptian researchers whose work is financed by foreign foundations or international organizations now work on topics that are often not of their own choice, or chosen by their own government, but by these foreign institutions. Much of the independence of researchers is inevitably lost in the process, not only in the researcher's choice of subject but even in the general orientation of the conclusions reached, since it is often obvious what conclusions the financing institution would like to see. The greater neutrality of research being done today is often more apparent than real.

When the era of emigration came in the mid-1970s, many Egyptian economists left for the Gulf, not to escape political oppression as they had in the late 1960s, but to escape economic decline. The impact of this latter-day migration on the economic profession in Egypt was worse than the earlier one, not only because it affected a much larger number of economists but also because on the whole, the demands of the jobs they went to were far less rigorous. Earlier migrants largely left Egypt to work in UN organizations or in countries where pay was more in proportion with qualification and responsibility than it was in the Gulf. As these migrants have returned from the Gulf, the effect of their having spent a number of years receiving a high pay for little productive work, is often negative.

I do not want to end this chapter on too pessimistic a note, nor is pessimism wholly warranted. It may be true that every generation has to carry a burden of its own and that there is no clear evidence that the new burdens

are any lighter than those of previous generations. The
generation of the inter-war period paid dearly for having
to study and write under colonial domination, even
though Egypt was nominally an independent country.
The post-war generation had to pay the price imposed by
the very persons who liberated the country from colonial
rule, the price being the very heavy hand of the state.
When this was lifted, the next generation bore the brunt
of an overly soft state. But none of this has prevented
significant progress from being made. Today, Egypt has
many more able economists than it had in 1920, many
more economics graduates, and far more economic statistics, conferences, journals, and publications of all kinds
as forums for debate and expression. For all this we
should be grateful to all three generations whatever their
shortcomings. Whether they wanted Egypt to remain
agricultural or to industrialize, whether they wrote economic history books, textbooks on economic theory, or
cost-benefit analyses, and whether they believed in 'laissez-faire,' cooperation, or socialism, most of them did
some good service to the economics profession. The
inevitable result was, of course, the growth of economic
knowledge. What is far less certain is whether, as we have
accumulated greater economic knowledge, we have also
grown more objective, more scientific, and less biased.
Just as one burden was substituted by another, so one
bias seems to have been replaced by another. The nationalist bias of the inter-war period was replaced by a bias
for socialism in the 1960s, followed in turn by a bias for
'laissez-faire.' We may have grown more skillful in hiding

our biases, or become less aware of them, but we are probably just as influenced by them as ever before. This may be the fate of all social scientists, in Egypt and elsewhere. What may be a more important cause for concern for specifically Egyptian economists is that their biases are becoming less and less their own, and more and more those imposed by outside influences.

14

Egypt and the Market Culture

A little more than half a century ago, the great British economic historian and sociologist Karl Polanyi published a book with the title *The Great Transformation*,[21] which achieved great fame and continues to be widely quoted. By "the great transformation," Polanyi meant a particular change that came over Europe a little more than two centuries ago. This was neither the emergence of capitalism, nor the acceleration of manufacturing, nor the rapid advance of science and technology, nor the beginning of the Enlightenment, but the emergence of 'the market system.' By 'the market system' Polanyi did not of course mean the familiar phenomenon of people gathering on a regular basis, in a certain place, to exchange a few basic goods, as seen in the weekly market in villages and small towns all over the world, which must be as old as the division of labor and the system of exchange. What he meant was the moment around the end of the eighteenth century and the beginning of the nineteenth, when the market engulfed such things as agricultural land and human labor which had not been considered marketable commodities until then. Polanyi considered this to be the true beginning of the economic system that prevails today, distinguishing it from any other economic system that Europe had known before the industrial revolution. Under this 'market system,' one thing after another came to be the object of a transaction of buying and selling, and hence to acquire monetary value. This trait, according to Polanyi, is of much greater significance than any trait that could distinguish capitalism from socialism, both capitalism and socialism being in fact two varieties of the 'market system.'

I personally find the idea fascinating and exceedingly fruitful, for it can throw strong light on some of the most important transformations in modern life, including those which have occurred in Egypt over the last fifty years. With the launching of Sadat's open-door policies in 1974, Egypt was bound to go through the same marketing fever that had affected everyone else. Thirty years ago, while spending a few months in Lebanon, I was struck by how much the city of Beirut looked like a huge commercial market, two thirds of the ground floor area of all buildings were estimated to be dedicated to selling one thing or another. Over the last three decades I could see the same thing gradually happening in Cairo. Anyone who has managed to get hold of the ground floor of a building has turned it into a commercial entreprise of some sort, and every young man in possession of any amount of capital thinks up a 'project,' which invariably means setting up an enterprise for marketing something.

During the 1950s and 1960s, the rate of growth of the market system in Egypt, in the sense I have suggested, was exceedingly slow for two main reasons. At that time, the government provided many of the essential goods and services at prices which virtually everyone could afford, while the rate of inflation was still very modest. Both factors helped to reduce the pressure that might have pushed people to search for sources of additional income. When essentials are available at reasonable prices and there is little fear of a big rise in prices in the near future, the buying and selling fever tends to abate, and so does the urge to make a big fortune in the shortest possible time.

By the mid-1970s, however, the situation had changed radically. With the sudden rise in prices after the upheaval in the oil market in the early seventies, the gradual reduction of government intervention for the protection of lower-income groups, and the flow of unprecedented wealth into the country from remittances, the market system heated up and the drive to realize a fortune by whatever means intensified. Things that had rarely been offered for sale or rent, as indeed they should never have been, came to be subject to negotiation. A good deal of public property became private, and hence

171

subject to buying and selling. Much of what everyone had enjoyed freely, such as public parks, beaches, or the banks of the Nile, was now transformed into building sites, either for profit or for the exclusive benefit of a limited group of people. Everyone began to look for new ways of earning more and more money, either out of necessity or in response to newly whetted appetites. He who had an apartment that he could rent to an Arab or foreign tourist, or had a private car that he could turn into a taxi to drive after finishing work in his government post, did exactly that. A school teacher who could offer private lessons after school hours (or even during them) did not hesitate to do so. The government employee entrusted with providing a public service at no charge turned it into a private service which he sold only to those able to pay, including certain functions connected with some highly sensitive posts in the government that no one would previously have imagined could be subject to the 'market system.' Sporting clubs began to cede more and more of their land and buildings, that had previously been set aside for their members' use, to commercial projects that aimed at nothing but profit. This is to say nothing of television, of course, where the opportunities for realizing profit are limitless. This powerful device, originally invented as a means of transmitting ideas and information, was transformed into a first-rate selling device in which advertising agencies came to control not only the timing but the very content of the programs.

With the increased opportunities for making large windfall profits, resulting from the big rise in the rate of inflation, and the inevitable increase in the intensity of desire for such profits, new types of aggressive and criminal behavior hardly known in Egypt before started to make an appearance. One would now try to put his hand on a lucrative plot of land which really belonged to someone else, another to supplant the legal owners or occupiers of a flat which promised a handsome income if appropriately furnished and rented to foreigners. A teacher might force private tuition on his students, at exorbitant rates, when they might have preferred a different tutor; a university professor might try to oust a colleague from teaching a particular course which offered rich rewards to the writer of its textbook, and so on.

As the years went by, I came to see how even the sacred month of Ramadan was gradually subjected to the rules of the market system, for it too was turned into an opportunity for intensive buying and selling. It is true that in my childhood, small lanterns were sold to children during Ramadan as one of the rituals of celebration, but these were only very simple, cheap toys, which the children used to carry as they gathered in the streets, singing the traditional Ramadan songs. Or, to use the terms which I previously employed, they were very inexpensive 'nouns' helping the children to perform a very enjoyable 'verb.' Today there are shops that sell nothing but Ramadan lanterns, in small and giant sizes, for the use of children as well as for the decoration of the entrances of big buildings or the lobbies of international hotels. They rarely carry candles, as was the case in my childhood, but are connected to electric wires or carry their own batteries.

Thus the Ramadan lantern is rapidly coming to occupy the same position as the Christmas tree in the West, converted from a beautiful religious symbol to an expensive and elaborate ritual around which revolves a great commercial fanfare. Very soon we will see the Ramadan lantern transformed into one of the essential pillars of the holy month of fasting, without which fasting itself may become incomplete and unacceptable. Once this is done, the 'market system' will have won a complete victory over some of the most intimate aspects of the everyday life of Muslims, as it had already done in the Christian West.

Some people may regard all these transformations in our way of life as merely the inevitable consequences of the adoption over the last three decades of open-door policies, or as no more than the familiar features of the capitalist system to which Egypt was converted after discarding the 'socialism' of the 1960s. Others may see them only as symptoms of a continuous process of westernization. Although there is truth in all of this, it may also be true that something more ominous is taking place. I personally am inclined to think that Karl Polanyi was right in putting so much emphasis on the emergence and spread of 'the market culture.' If this is as applicable to Egypt as it is elsewhere, it would mean that we are now witnessing the gradual encroachment of something much more sinister than open-door policies, capitalism, or westernization. It could be nothing less than a process of metamorphosis in which everything is gradually being turned into a commodity, the object of a commercial transaction, including man's very soul.

Notes

1. G. Abd al-Khalek and R. Tignor, eds., *The Political Economy of Income Distribution in Egypt*, New York: Holmes and Meier, 1982.

2. *Ibid*, p. 398.

3. P. Sorokin, *Social and Cultural Mobility* (1927), Illinois: The Free Press of Glencoe, 1959, pp. 565–68.

4. It is thus not difficult to explain the great success enjoyed by films such as *Khalli bâlak min Zuzu* (Keep an Eye on Zuzu) in the mid-1970s, or the television serial *Rihlat al-milyun* (The Million-Dollar Journey) in the mid-1980s, where the heroine in the former and the hero in the latter both succeed in making a great move up the social ladder and in gaining the sympathy of the audience. During the same period (1975 to 1985) the most popular play, both in the theater and in television, was the play *Madrasat al-mushaghibin* (The School of Troublemakers), with its mockery by the pupils—who bear all the signs of belonging to a lower but rising class—of a headmaster and a teacher, both of whom belong to the middle class which has begun to suffer decline. The subject of the students' mockery ranges from the teacher speaking in classical Arabic, to her attention to philosophical issues and her demand for discipline.

5. See Charles Issawi, *Egypt in Revolution*, Oxford: Oxford University Press, 1963, pp. 118 and 156.

6. See A. Barakat, *al-Milkiya al-zira'iya bayn thawratayn, 1919–1952*, Cairo: al-Ahram Centre for Political and Strategic Studies, 1978, p. 61.

7. S. Ibrahim, "Egypt's Islamic Militants," in N. Hopkins and S. Ibrahim, eds., *Arab Society: Social Science Perspectives*,

Cairo: The American University in Cairo Press, 1987. Originally published in *MERIP Reports*, no. 103, 1982.

8. *Ibid.*, p. 503.

9. A. Hourani, *A History of the Arab Peoples*, London: Faber and Faber, 1991, p. 340.

10. Egyptian social and cultural life has also witnessed the appearance of figures playing a prominent role in the mass media and with wide popular appeal, who are strongly reminiscent of Molière's *Tartuffe*, a phenomenon with hardly any parallel in the 1960s. The combination of Tartuffe's false religiosity and materialistic greed seems to flourish more in certain social environments than in others and it is a fact that Molière's *Tartuffe* was a straightforward comment on an important social phenomenon of the time. There is also some evidence to suggest that the 'Tartuffes' of later seventeenth-century France were largely to be found among a new, recently enriched 'rentier' class. (see, for instance, L. Lough, *An Introduction to 17th-Century France*, London: Longman Green Co., 1954, pp. 41–42).

11. This was the main theme in Naguib Mahfouz's novel *Ahl al-qimma* (People at the Top), published in the early 1970s, which skillfully portrayed the feelings of humiliation and frustration that hounded an honest police officer who found himself incapable of protecting his sister from falling into the snare of a sharp-witted and energetic, but not completely honest businessman.

12. G. Hamdan, *Shakhsiyat Misr*, Alam al-Kutub, 1, 1980, p. 241.

13. *Ibid.*, p. 43.

14. This was published as a special issue of *L'Egypte Contemporaine*, the journal of the Egyptian Society for Political Economy, Statistics, and Legislation, Cairo, 1950.

15. In 1924, Tal'at Harb was invited to be the guest speaker in

the annual graduation ceremony of the American University in Cairo. Looking for a theme for his speech, he found it suitable to compare AUC with Bank Misr, of which he was the proud father. He said that in two respects at least, Bank Misr and AUC were similar: both were four years old and both were created to teach 'self-reliance' to Egyptians. In the case of Bank Misr, he said this was done despite the skepticism of many who believed that Egyptians could not, by their very nature, become good accountants, and that accounting would always remain an 'imported profession' in Egypt. *Magmu'at khutub Tal'at Harb*, Cairo: Matba'at Misr, 1927, pp. 82–83.

16. A. Crouchley, *The Economic Development of Modern Egypt*, London: Longman, 1939.

17. B. Hansen and G. Marzouk, *Development and Economic Policy in the UAR (Egypt)*, Amsterdam: North Holland Co, 1965.

18. P. O'Brien, *The Revolution in Egypt's Economic System*, Oxford: Oxford University Press, 1966.

19. See for instance Louis Awad, "Cultural and Intellectual Developments in Egypt since 1952," in P. Vatikiotis, ed., *Egypt since the Revolution*, London: Allen & Unwin, 1968.

20. H. Riade, *L'Egypte Nasserienne*, Paris: Les Editions de Minuit, 1964.

21. K. Polanyi, *The Great Transformation: The Political and Economic Origins of Our Time* (1944), Boston: Beacon Press, 1957.